Art, Art, Art! Before Words: Volume Two

Emily Sturgill

2014

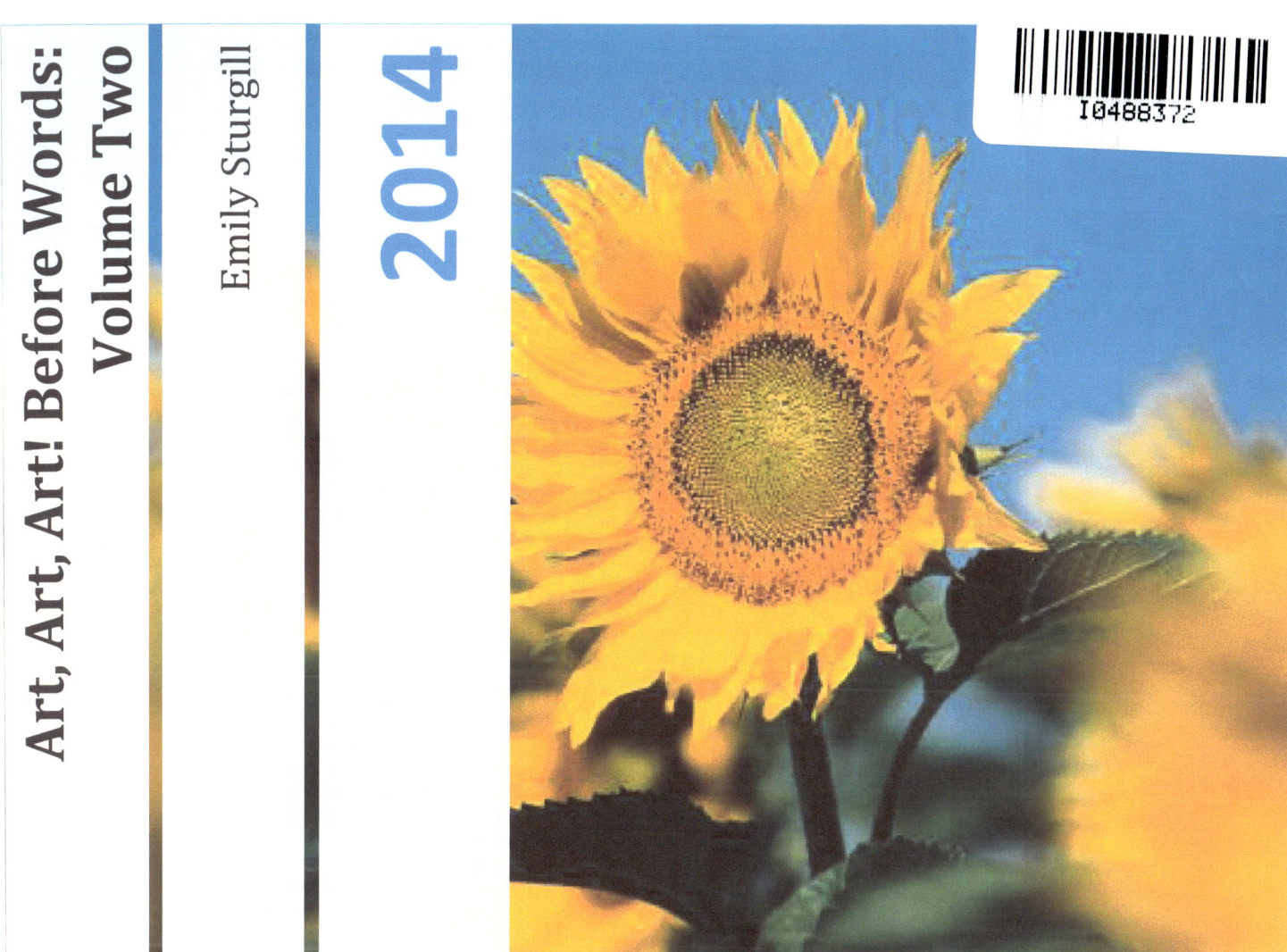

This book contains all original Artwork by Artist Emily H. Sturgill. This is the second Volume of her collected Artworks. It is a wide spectrum of her art over a period of many years.

From the Creator of:
Sex in the kitchen sink
A WordPress.com blog
http://sexinthekitchensink.wix,com/books-
by-emily

Preface-3/15/14

Saturday Evening 8:45PM EST.

The Artist is also an Art Therapist, and a published Poetess. She has made art her entire life starting at the age of four years old. She was diagnosed with severe mental illness just after graduating high school in 1992. She was just 18 years old. Emily decided instead of allowing her manic-depressive disorder to control and limit her life, she would continue to try her best to deal with the cards she was dealt. She attended college part-time for many years, beginning with general studies at Macomb Community College in Warren Mi. She attended from Fall 1993-Fall 1997. At that time she transferred to the much larger Wayne State University in Detroit Michigan.

Despite warnings and objections from both of her parents, Emily pursued her dreams of Fine Art. She earned a Bachelors Degree of Fine Arts with a concentration-(major)-in Painting. She received her degree after 13 years of undergraduate studies. It was at this time that her live in and loyal long term boyfriend, Dean encouraged Emily to apply to graduate school. Emily had dreams for many years of becoming an Art Therapist. In May 2006 Emily earned her BFA. That spring she applied to Wayne State's Art Education & Art Therapy-(M.Ed) program. She was accepted and enrolled in the Fall of 2006. It took her longer than most, but after almost 6 years she graduated from the program and was awarded a Masters Degree in Art Education with a core concentration-(focus)-in Art Therapy.

Milestones-

1992-being diagnosed bipolar and receiving a high school dipolma.

1993-began community college

1993,1996,1999-had solo art shows at local coffeehouses.

2000-met future husband and live in boyfriend Dean Sturgill

2002-began acceptance of my bipolar illness

2003-2007 in active recovery of my illness

2006-graduated with BFA

2007-awarded first scholarship for Art Therapy

2007-had major episode of Mania.

2007-2010-no more major episodes bipolar was in remission

2010-had a reoccurence of Major bipolar Depression

2011-got married after 11 years of dating my live in boyfriend Dean.

2011-after honeymoon was over quickly had a series of small hypomanias.

2012-graduated with my Masters of Art Education & Art Therapy.

2012- Started my blog on WordPress.com called "Sex in the kitchen Sink."

This was my 3rd or 4th attempt at blogging. But this time was different, instead of a typical blog-I merely wrote poetry. That was the bare bones basis of my blog and remains so to this day. I now have roughly 257 followers-or subscribers, (readers)-of my little blog.

2012-2013-I sought employment for over a year and a half as an art therapist.

2013-published 11 poetry and artist chapbooks through Amazon's Kindle Direct Self-publishing platform.

I also published my personal Memoirs of living with bipolar disorder-"Memoirs Recalled Madness: a personal account of living with manic-depressive illness." Currently I have released a 4th edition. I needed to revise so many times, due to not being that type of Author. I also released my first collection of stand alone Artworks, called, "Art before words. Volume One." -2013. By Emily Sturgill.It was part of a two part series I called,

"Art, Art, Art!!! Before Words." This is the second edition to that series.

I hope you enjoy the artwork and images, creations -I guess that I could call them that? That, I have included in this book. While I tried to not duplicate the art from the first collection into this collection, it would not surprise me one bit if I goof up and do do that. As an artist who has been making art almost complusively for well over three decades, I have a lot of artwork to catolog & attempt to keep track of.

This book would never be possible without all the perks of being married to one really cool,groovy and awesome guy. Dean has done nothing but shown me encouragement, love and support throughout our almost 14 year long relationship. He was the one who motivated me to apply to grad school-I was terrified. And he was also the one, who convinced me to finish my BFA to begin with. Without Dean always beside me-cheering me on-I doubt I ever would have self-published a single page of anything at all. Talent means nothing if you do not believe in yourself. It's also equally meaningless, if you cannot trust yourself or accept yourself. You never know what is possible if you do not try.They do say that every journey begins with one single step-this is something I know is very much true. Every journey of the path you are on-it will always begin the same way with a single step.

I hope you enjoy your path and your journey. But for now, I encourage you to take that first single step but this time into my world! There are things to see, stories to tell, not with words by before words with images. Here take a deep breath and step into the great unknown of my crazy little world of Art. Art before Words.

Sincerely,

Emily Sturgill.

Table of Contents

PAINTING WITH FIRE-

By Emily Sturgill

2/12/13

I paint sometimes

Like I am on Fire and I cannot

Put out the flame.

I just burn.

And the images, color the canvas,

Like some sort of wicked magic.

It's my desire that burns...

To release some sort of image,

Trapped within me.

And I never quite know where,

to start. I begin with a background-and-then,

in my Randomness, I create Art.

It is something quick and jumpy, like,

a rabbit freaking out, because it is scared.

I frequently paint like I am on Fire.

Just one quick session, 2-3 hours, without any plans.

Yet, somehow, I know:

I always land on my feet smothered in paint-

Not burns.

Just imagery, making a mess of me,

Yet again.

SHAKESPEARE-

"For he should make the face of heaven so fine,

that all the world be in love with night."-Romeo and Juliet

Shooting stars

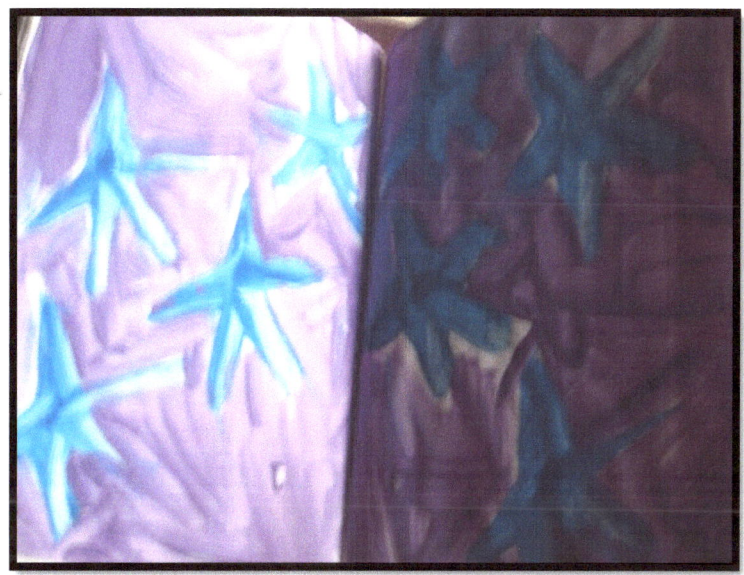

cover my lover blindly

as night descends so rapidly

rapid, rapid, rapid

rapidly like semi-automatic gunfire

the sky falls down

to swallow us whole

into blackened night.

shooting stars,

but the only light i see

is in my lovers bright beautiful wide blue eyes...

purple skies

for purple stars of creamy bright

and shattering light.

then sooner

than light, Dawn creeps her way in.

She shadows us by pouring sunlight

into each and every crack

upon my lovers tattooed back.

Dawn does come

and she is bringing

the Sun.

you better run fast

faster then the Sun

if you wish to ignore Dawns pleas

and cries.

if your only desperate longing,

is to revisit last night's

shooting stars

and the snarl of the peaceful net-

the web of sleep

the spider of dreams.

"For he should make the face of heaven so fine,

    that all the world be in love with night."-Romeo and Juliet

Shooting stars

cover my lover blindly

as night descends so rapidly

rapid, rapid, rapid

rapidly like semi-automatic   *gunfire*

the sky falls down

to swallow us whole

into blackened night.

> "Doubt thou the stars are fire;
> Doubt that the sun doth move;
> Doubt truth to be a liar;
> But never doubt I love."
> — William Shakespeare, *Hamlet*

2002, Digital photography, "Buddha and Crayons." by Emily H. Cato-(Sturgill)

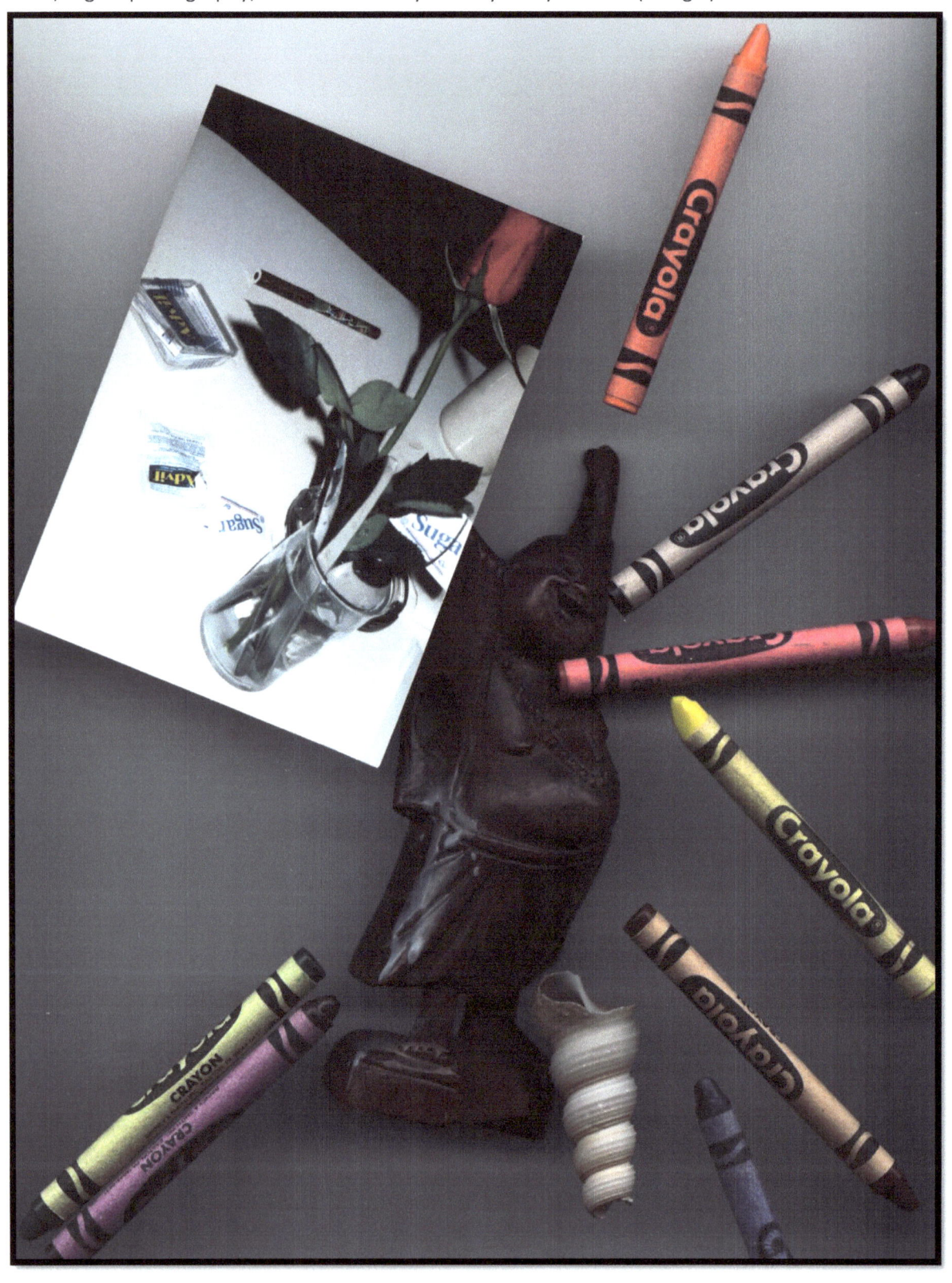

2010, Flower mixed media tissue-paper project, by Emily H.Cato(Sturgill)

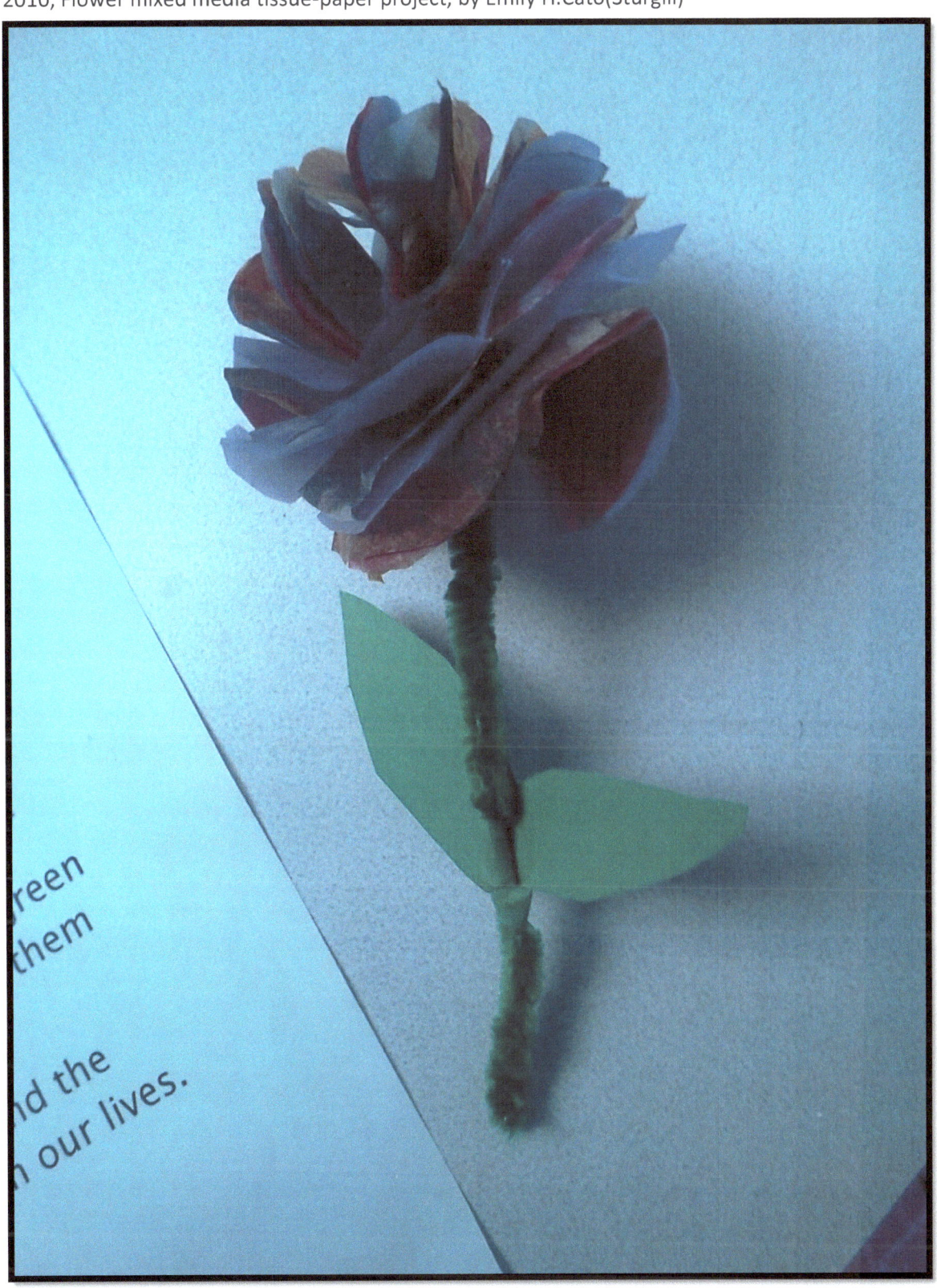

2010.Inside/OutsideBox,mixed media by Emily H.Cato (Sturgill)

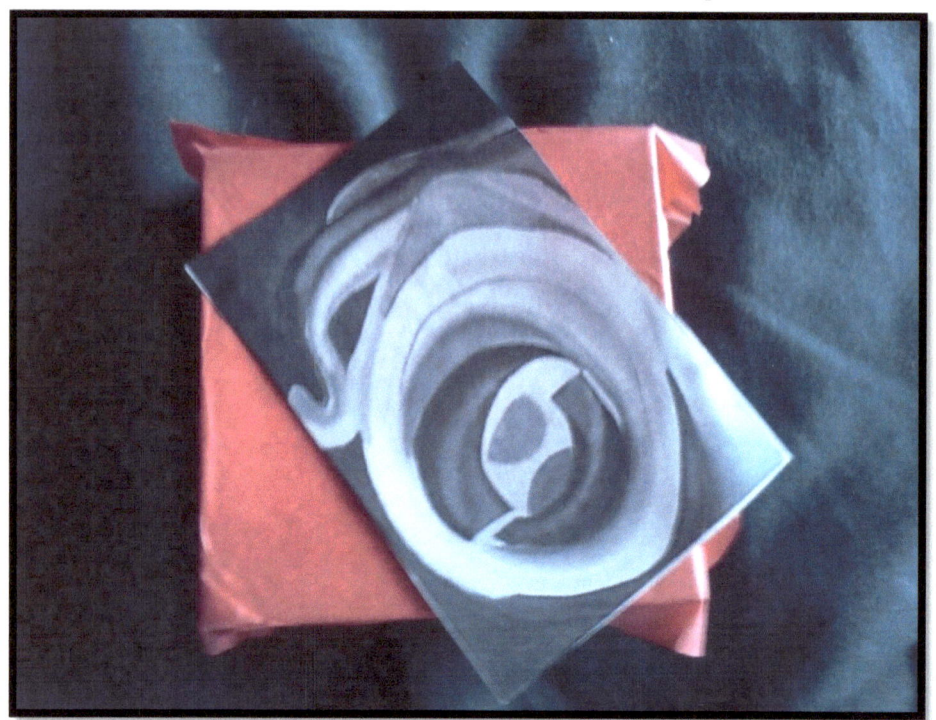

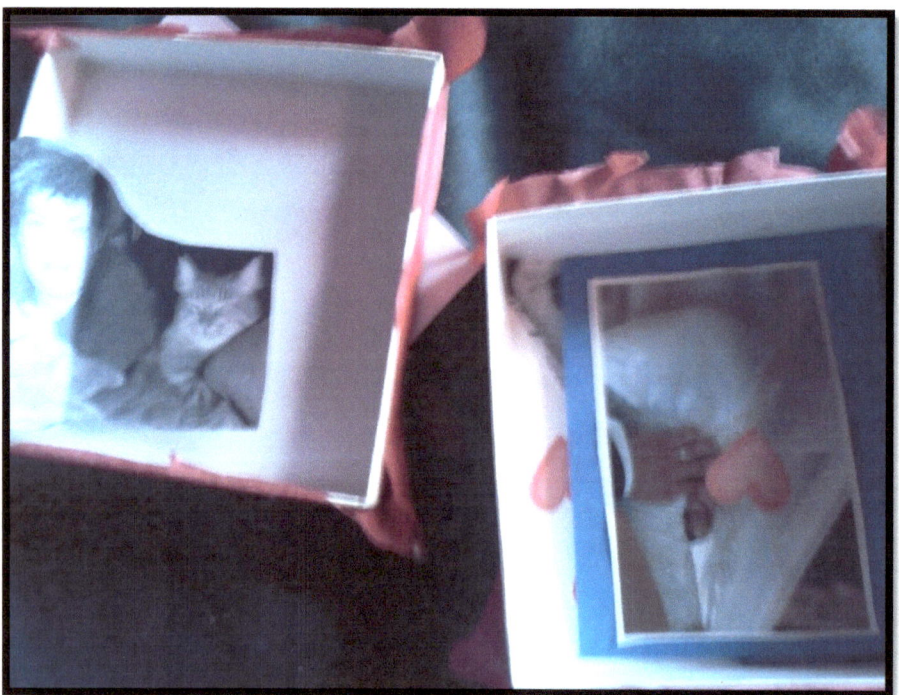

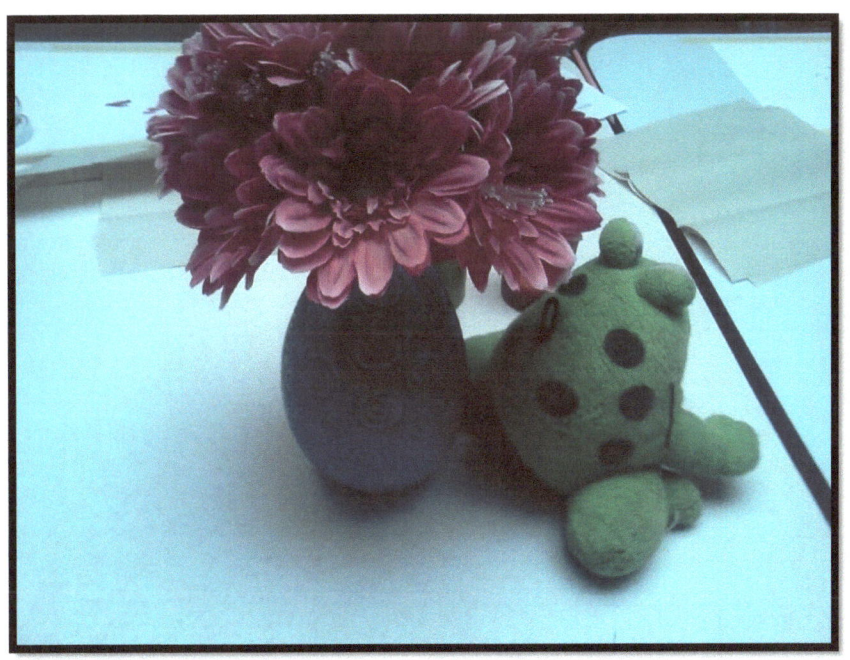

2010. Simple still-life, for elderly clients, watercolor example by Emily H.Cato (Sturgill.)

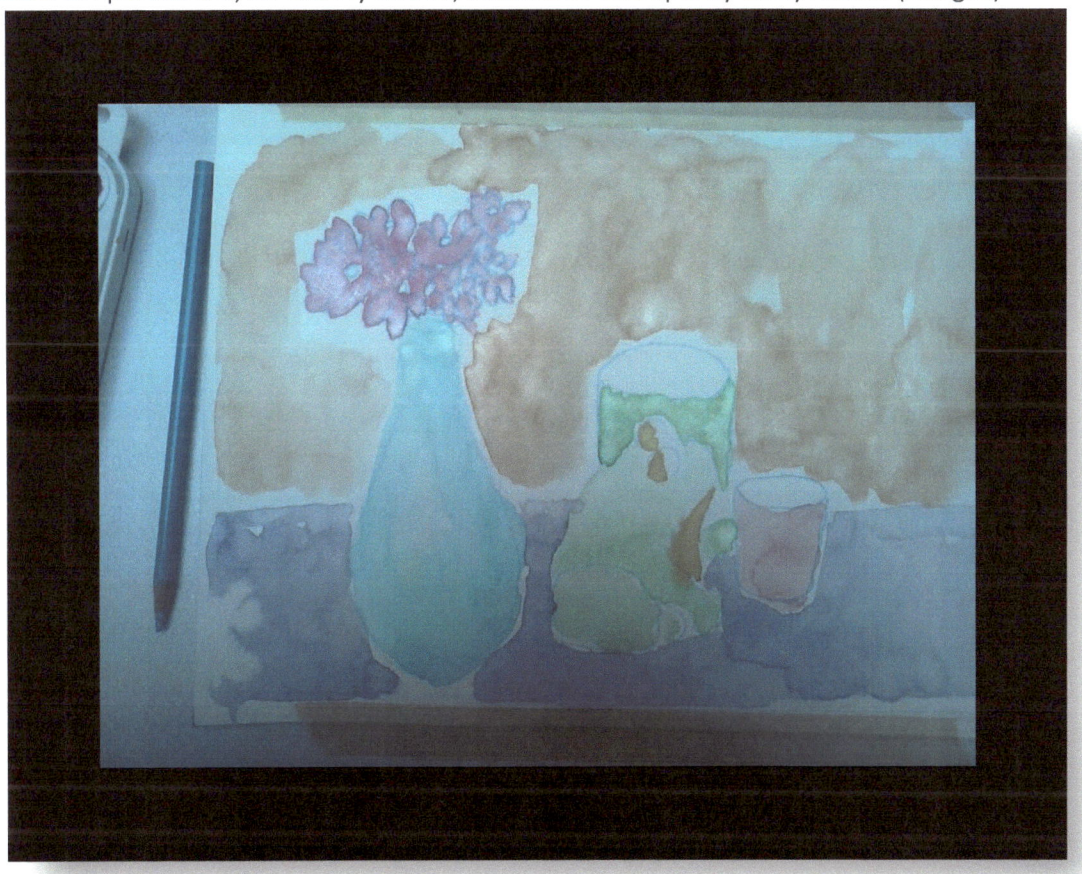

2002, basic photography project, 35 mm Camera "Detroit Landscape" by Emily H. Cato (Sturgill)

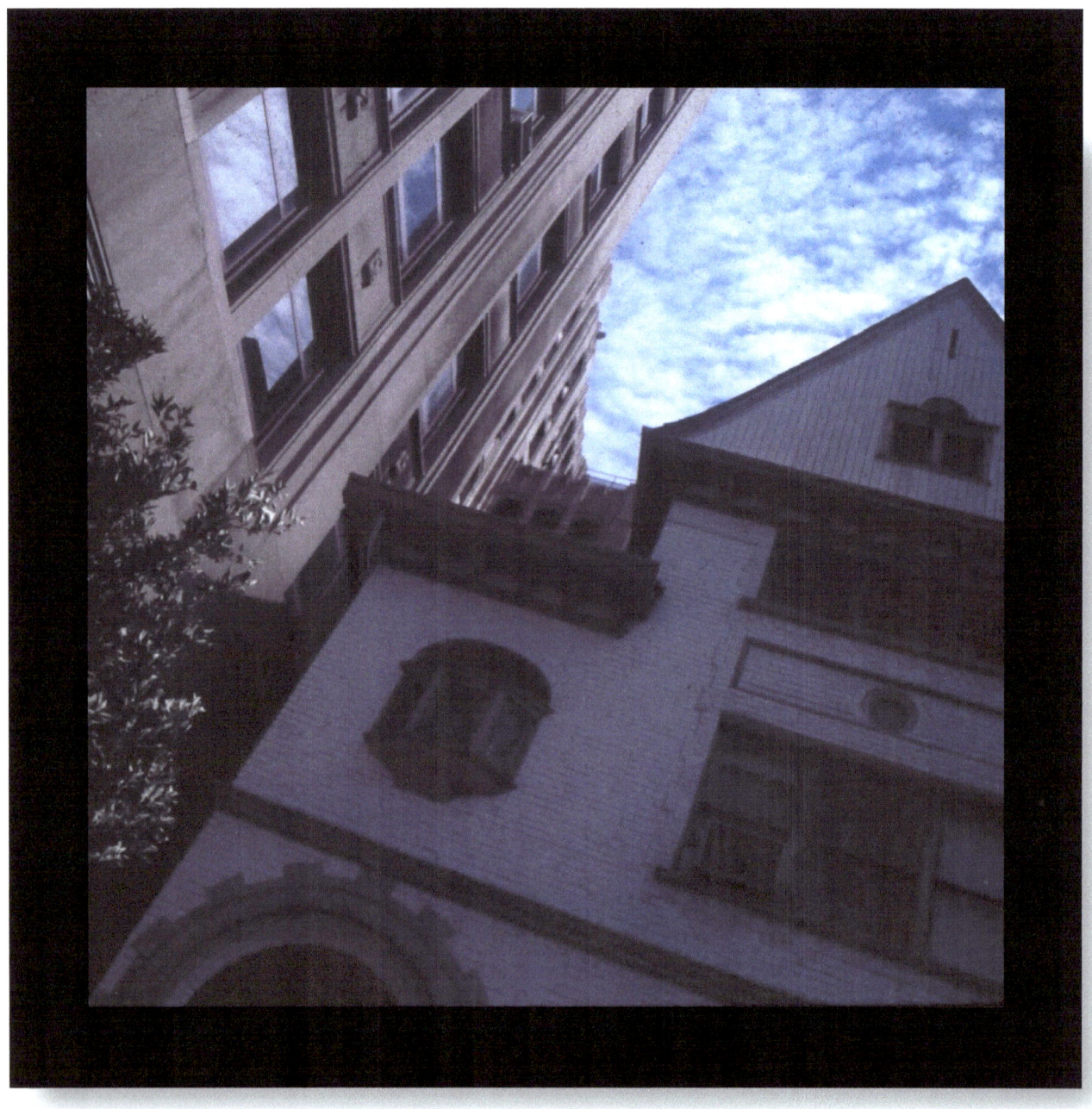

2002. "Building No.2" Photography, Detroit landscape.By Emily H.Cato(Sturgill)

2002.Color photography & digital effects. "Building No.3."by Emily H.Cato(Sturgill)

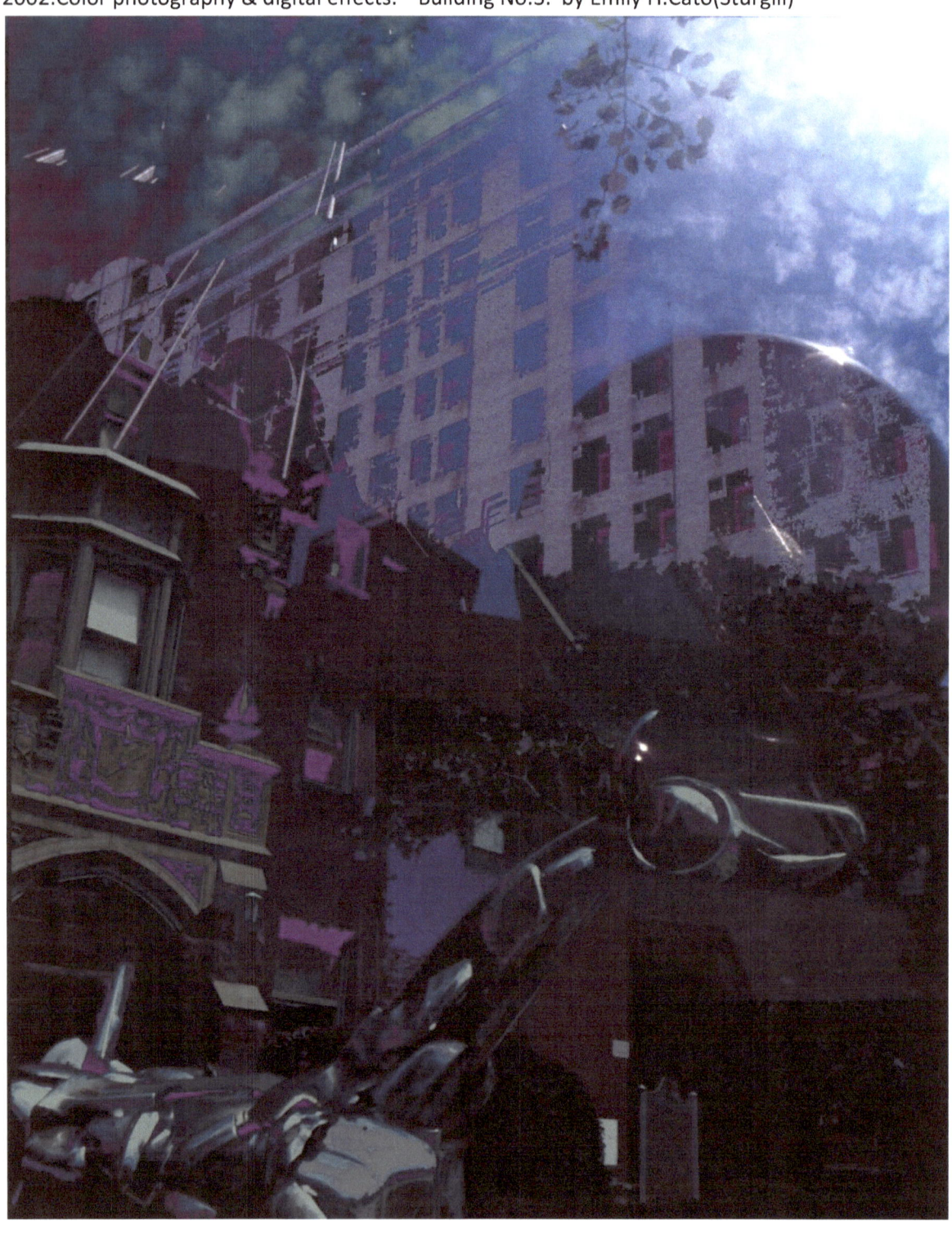

2002.Digital photography by Emily H.Cato.(Sturgill)- "Church".

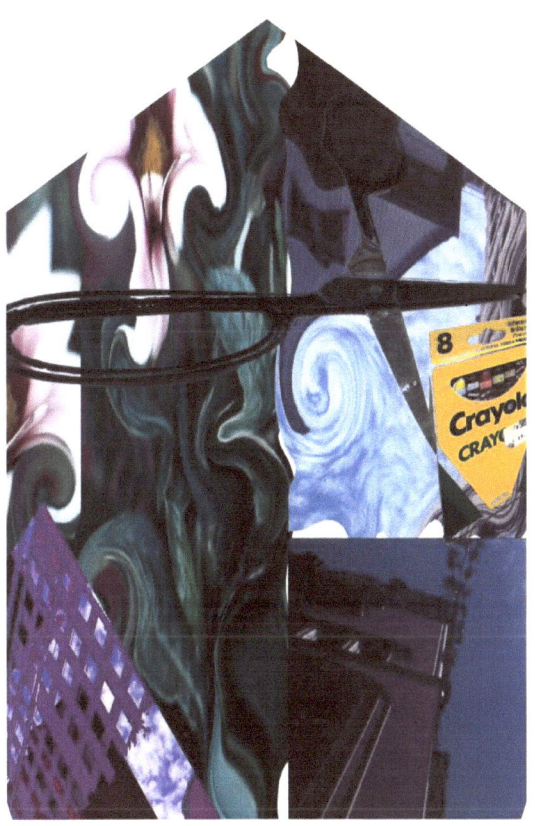

1998.Pen and ink drawing. "The tangled thread." Emily H. Cato(Sturgill)

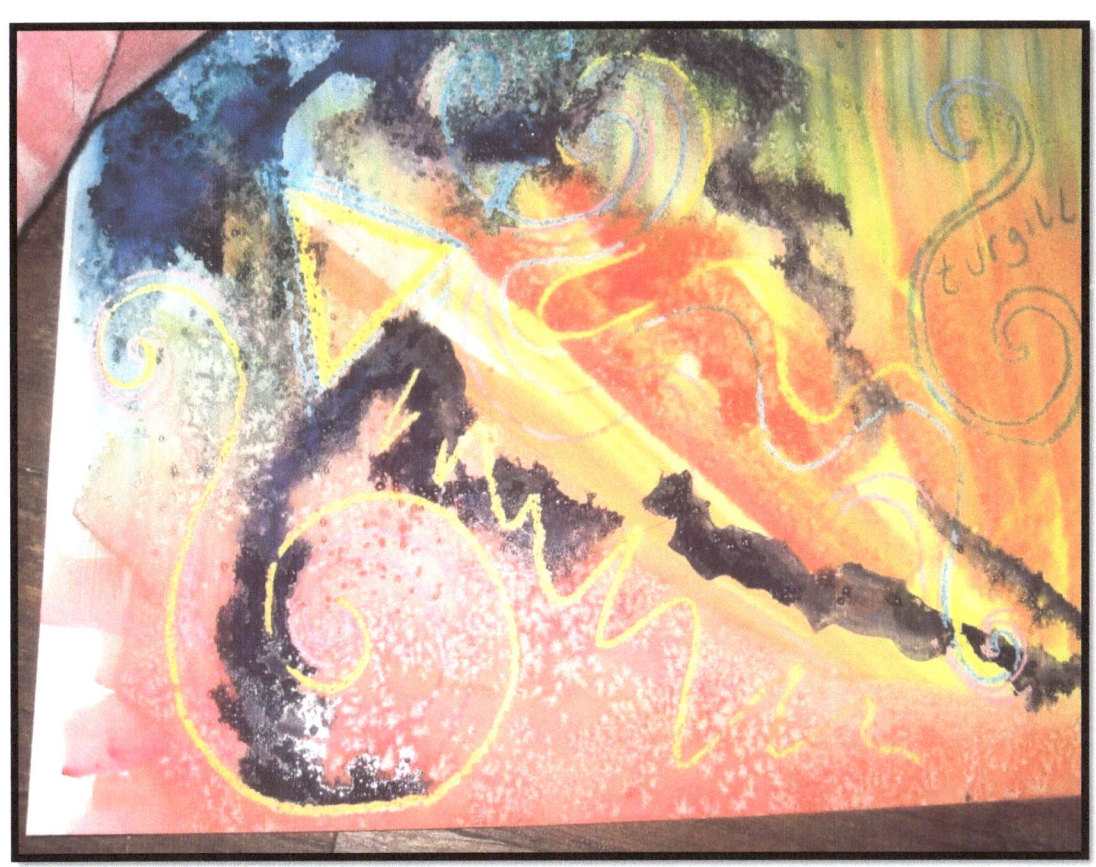

2012. "Abstraction Sturgill No.1" Salt, Crayon & Watercolor Resist. Emily H. Sturgill.

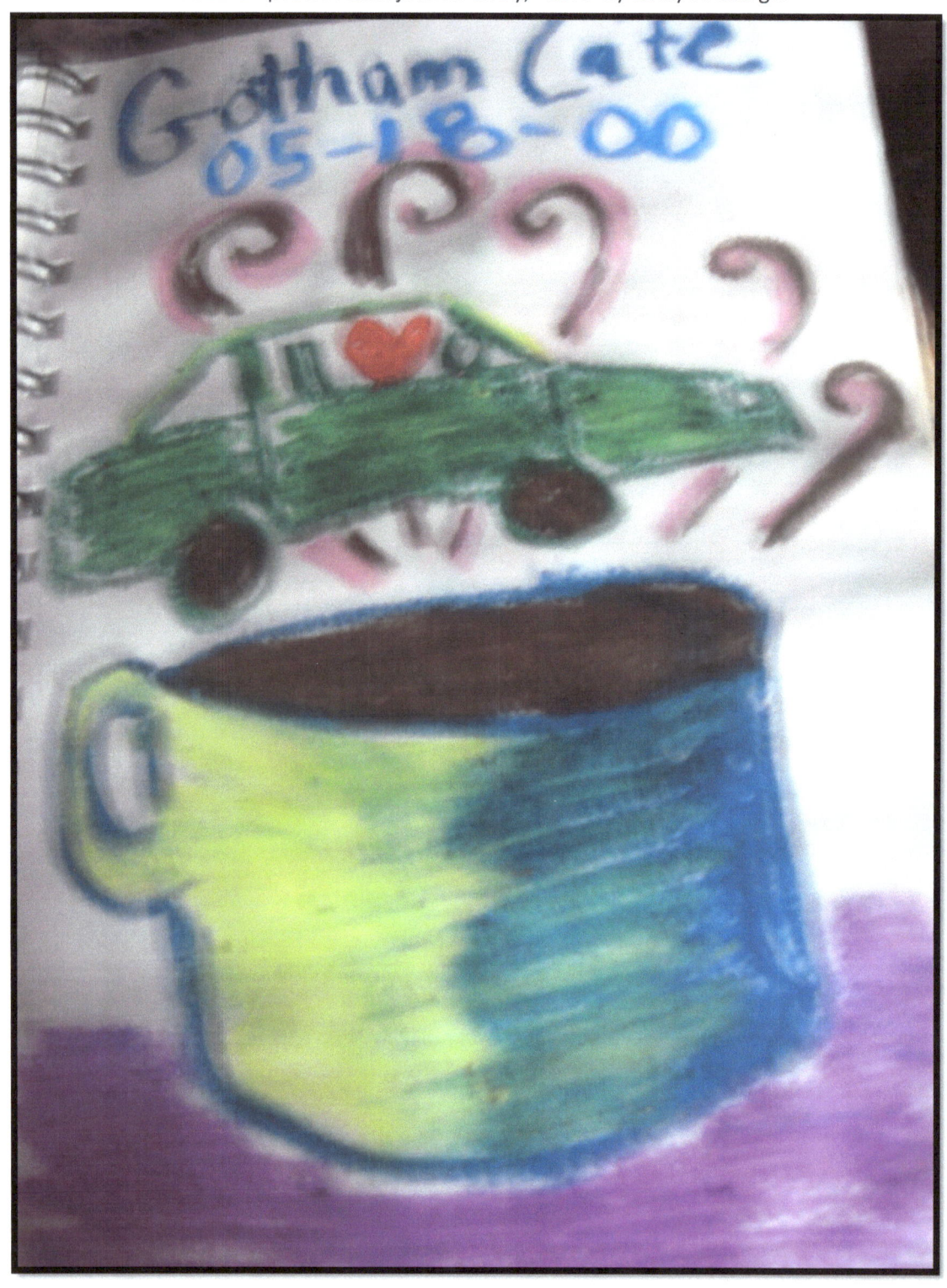

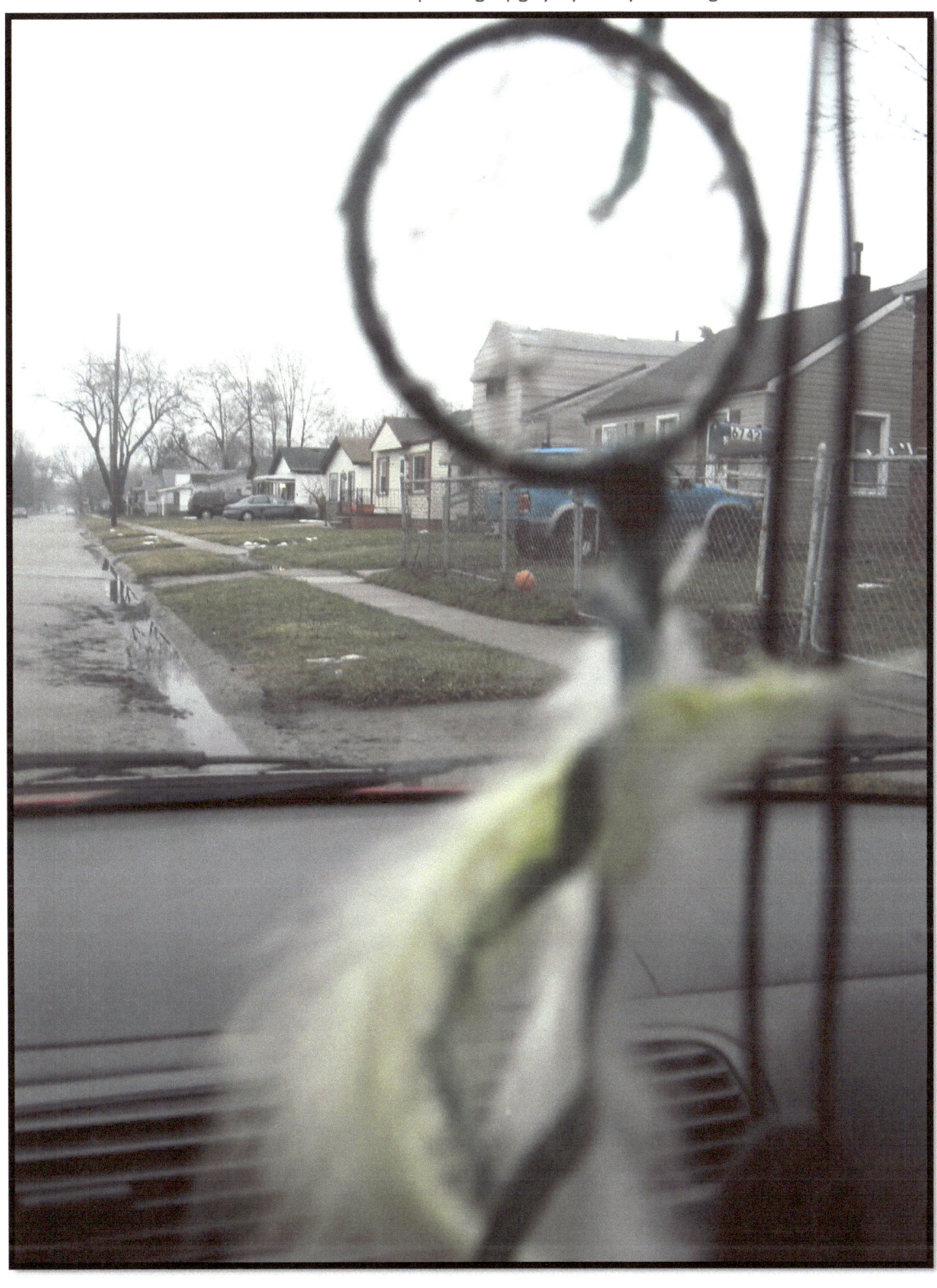

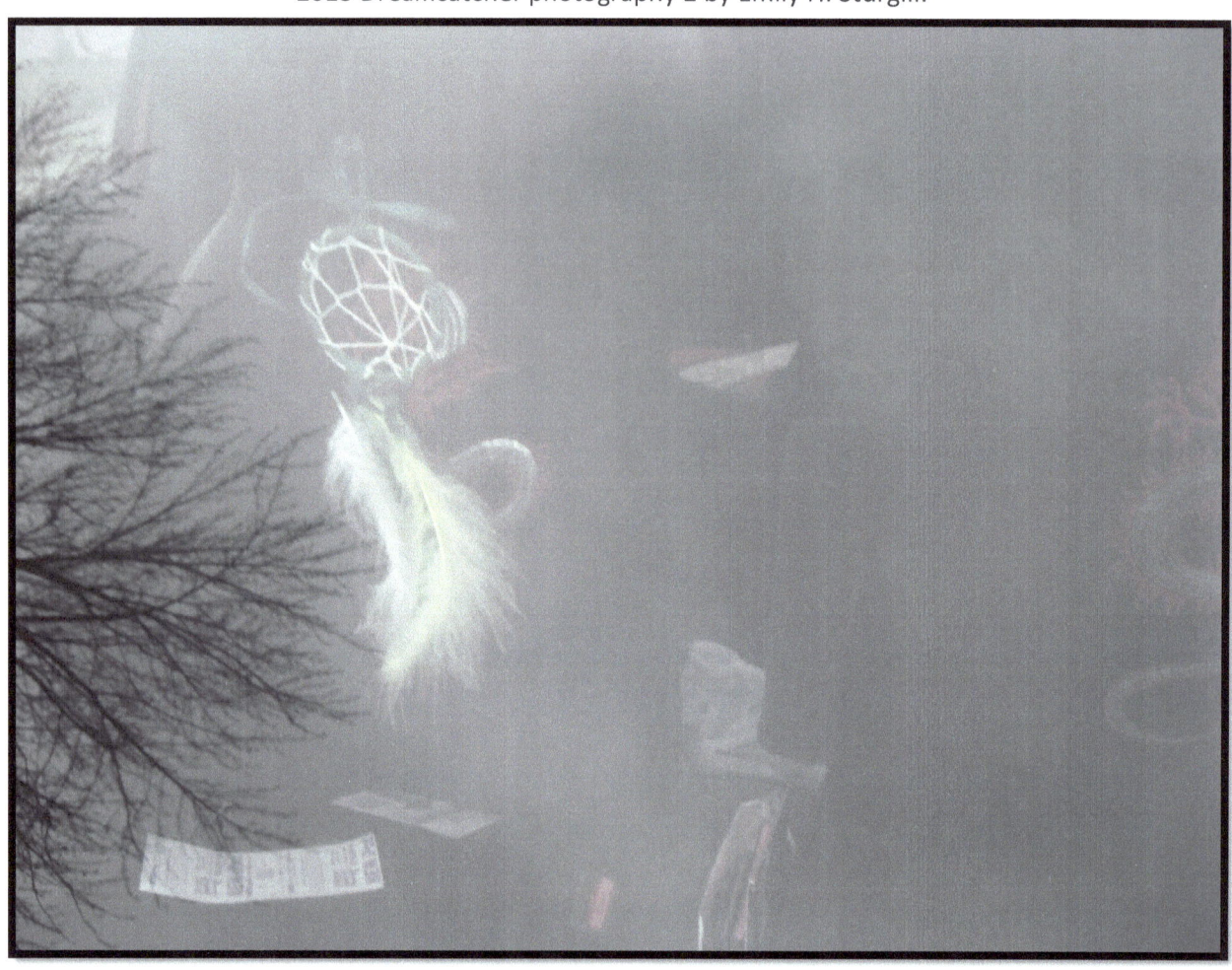

1999.Drawing mixed media. "Dream"by Emily H. Cato (Sturgill)

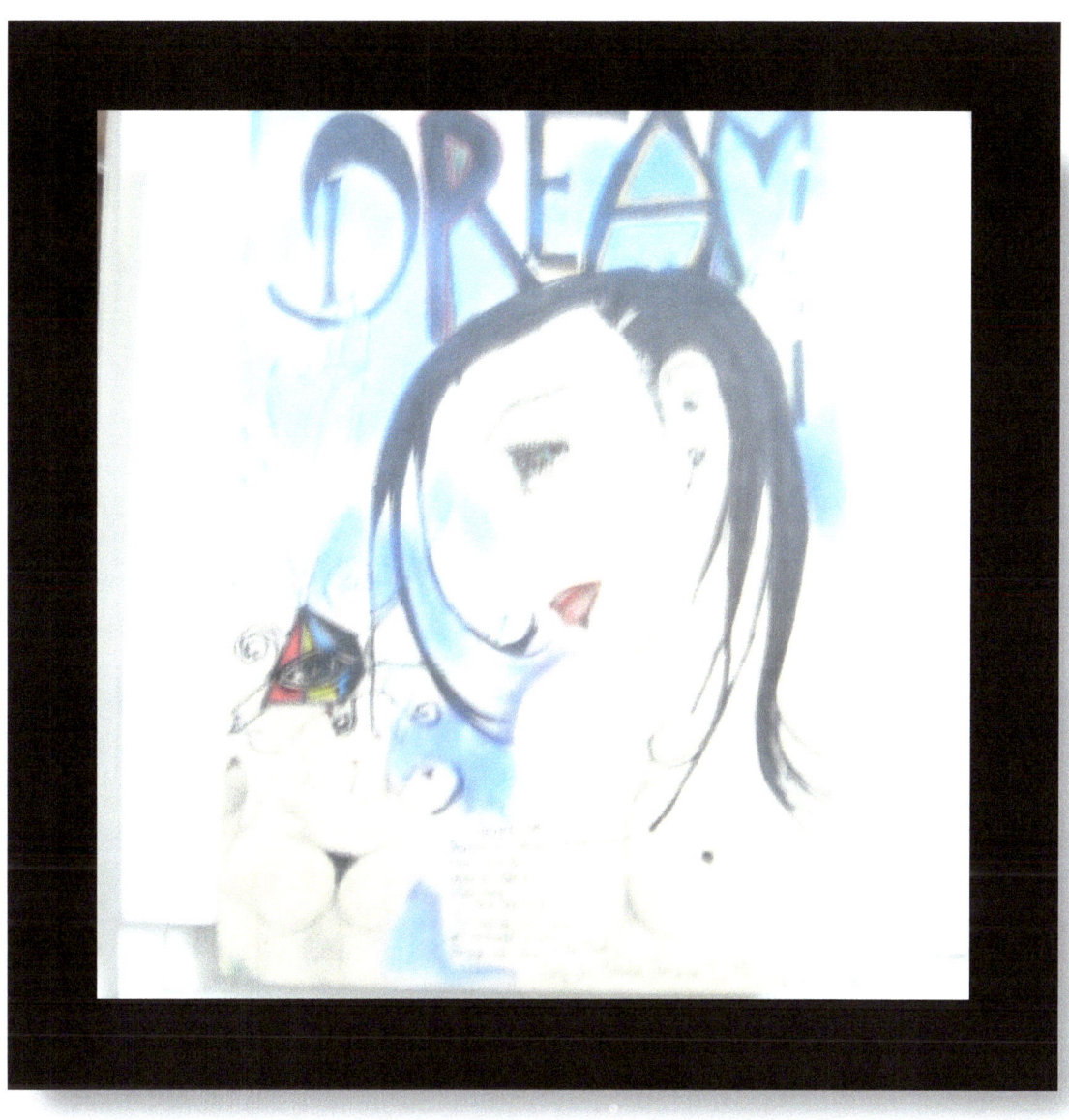

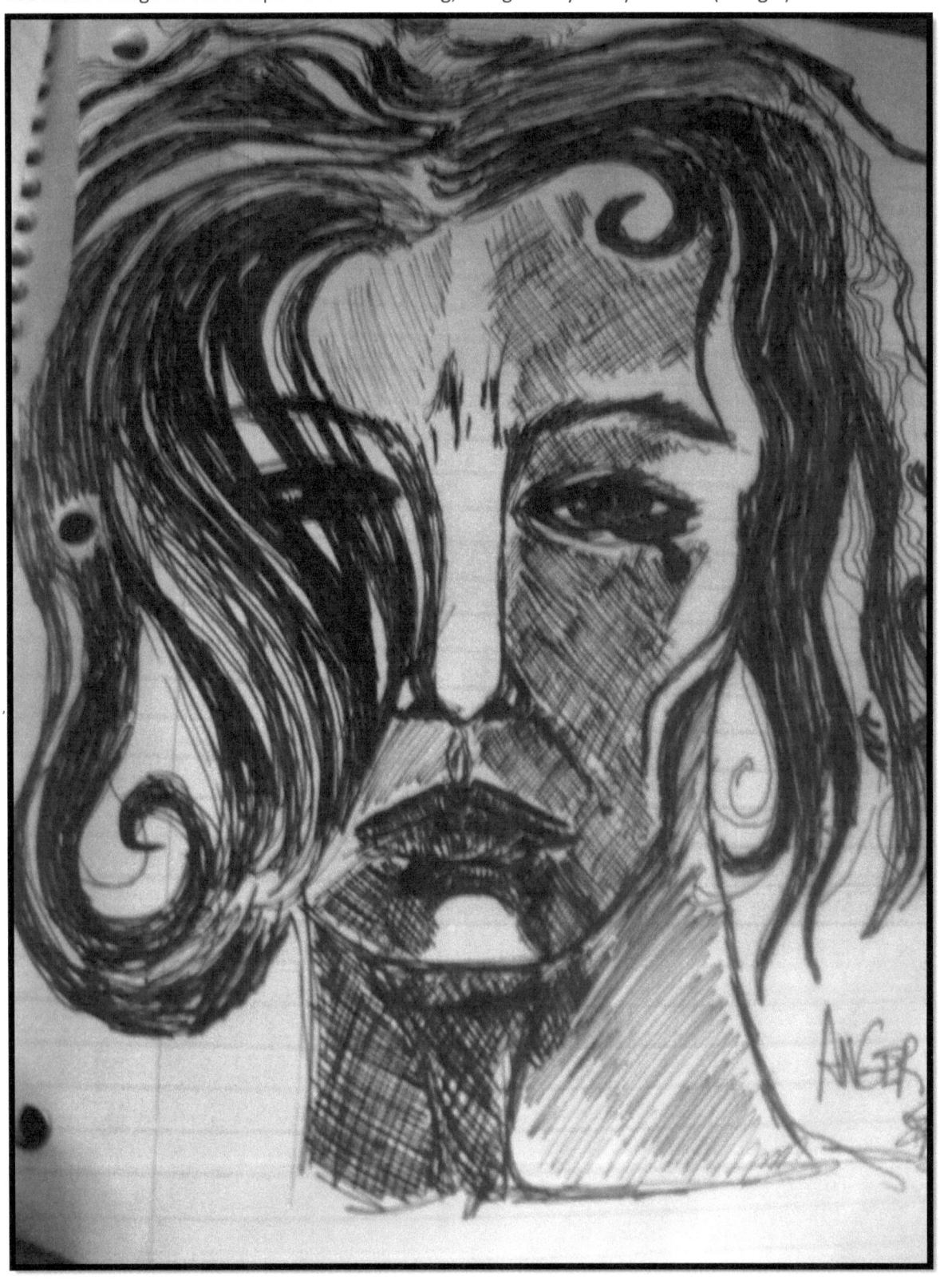

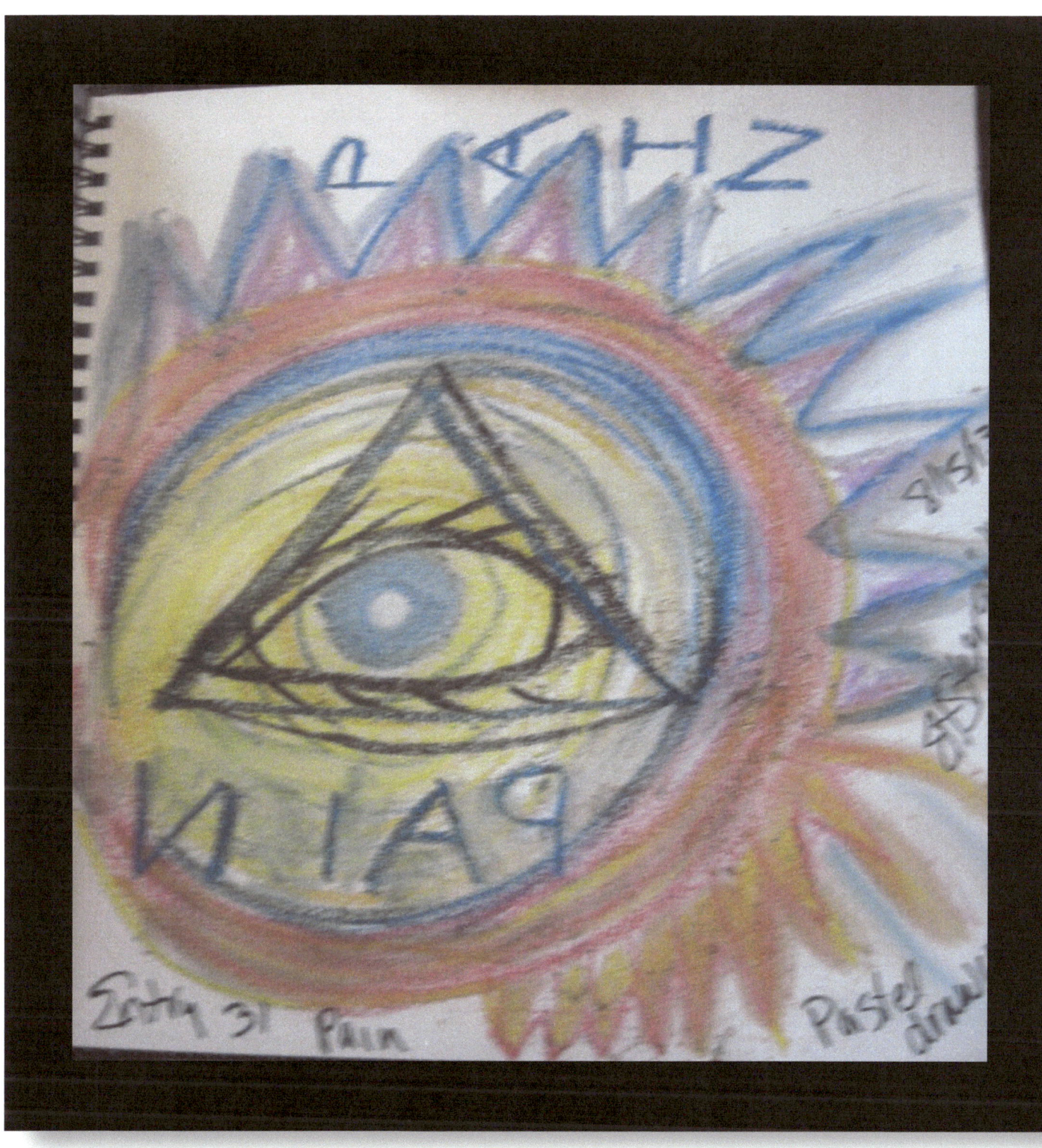

2002. Digital photography. "Cats." by Emily H. Cato (Sturgill)

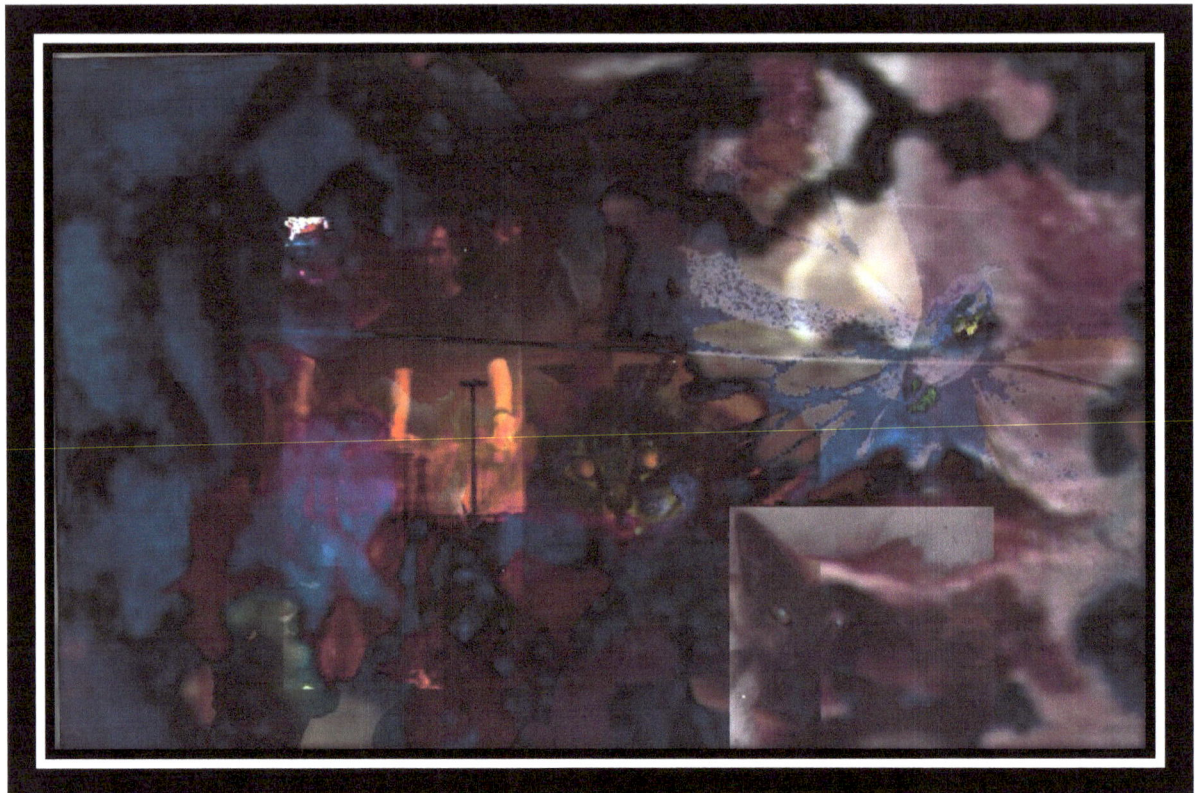

2012.Watercolor & mixed media, homemade birthday card for my husband Dean. By Emily H. Sturgill.

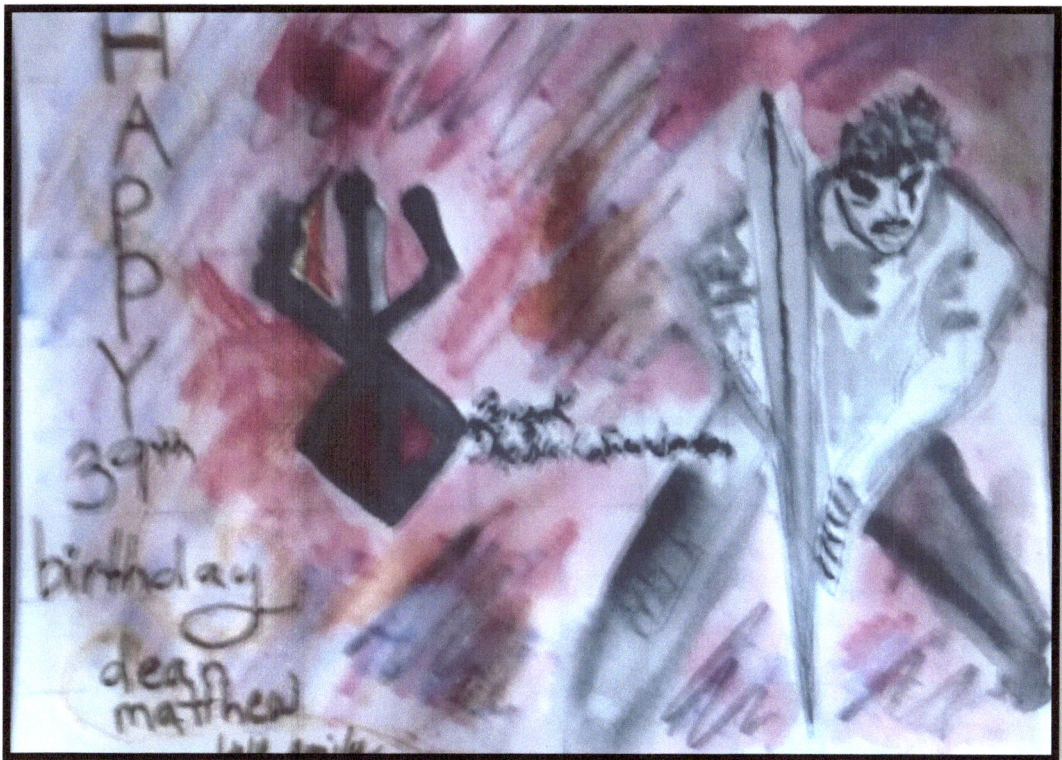

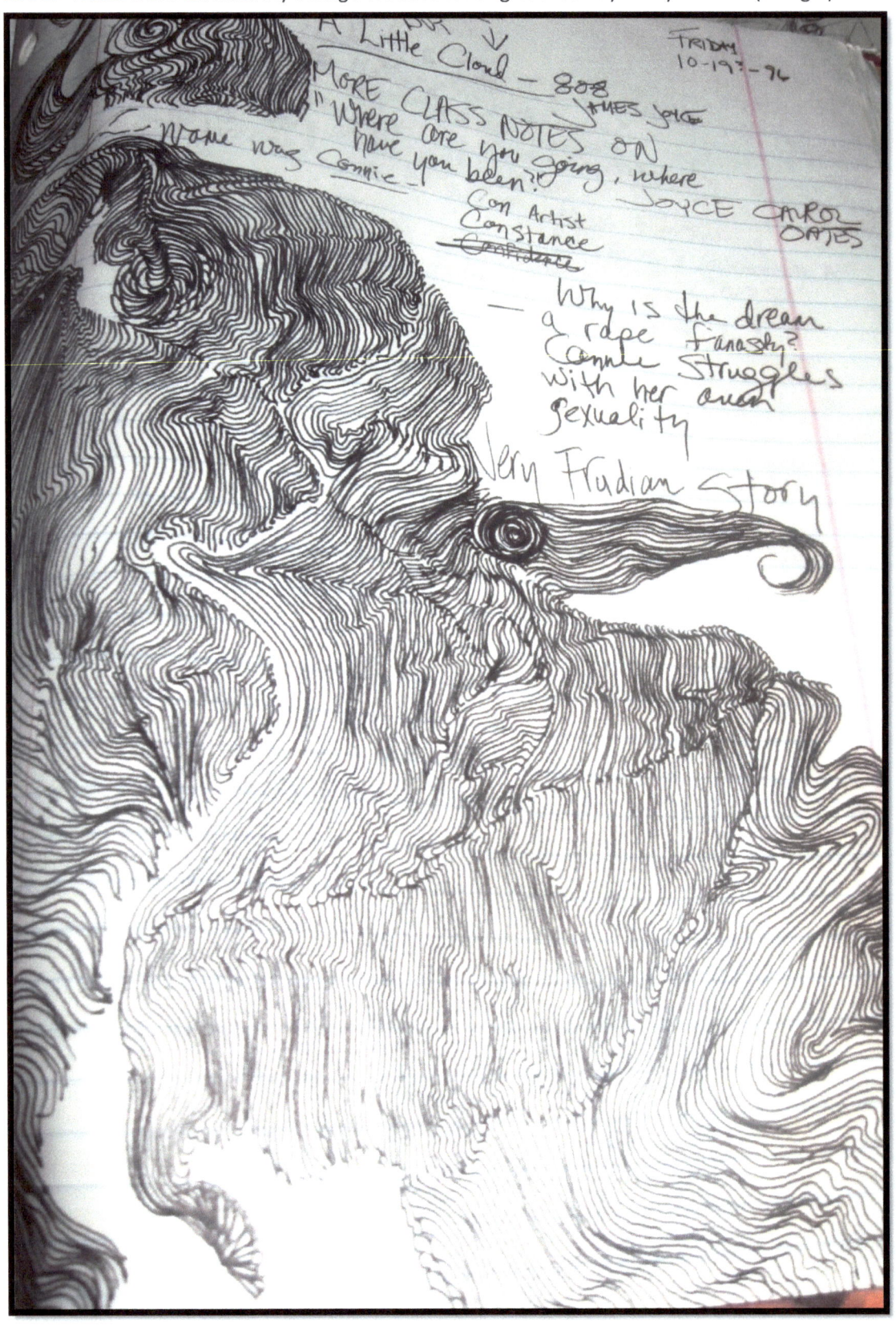

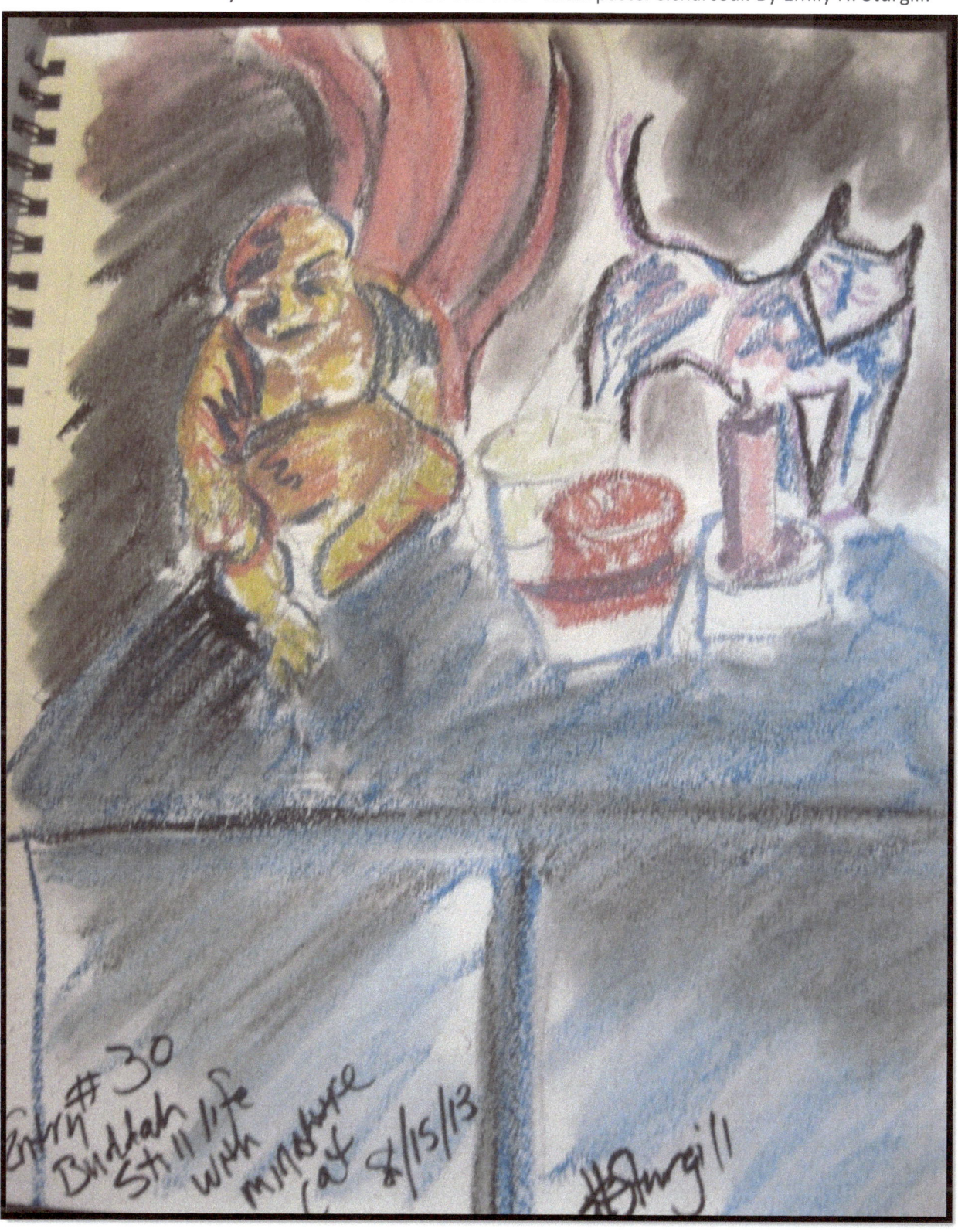

1998. "Battered Lizards remain Psychic." Mixed media, acrylic paint,newspaper,gesso and acrylic art gel medium. By Emily H. Cato-(Sturgill) on display in Fall 1999 at Gotham Coffeehouse, Ferndale

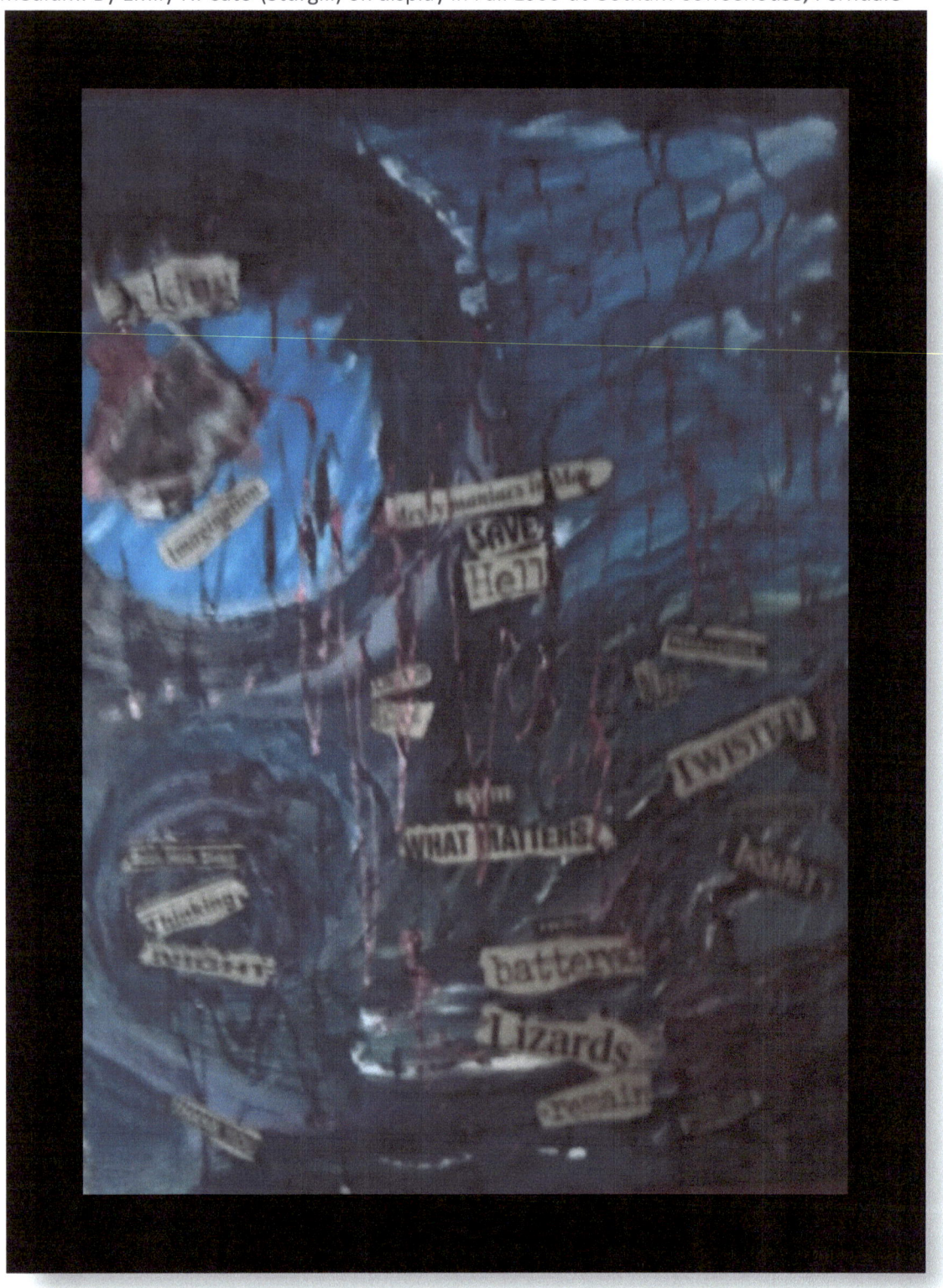

2002.Digital photography. "Detroit Lions at the Zoo." by Emily H. Cato-(Sturgill)

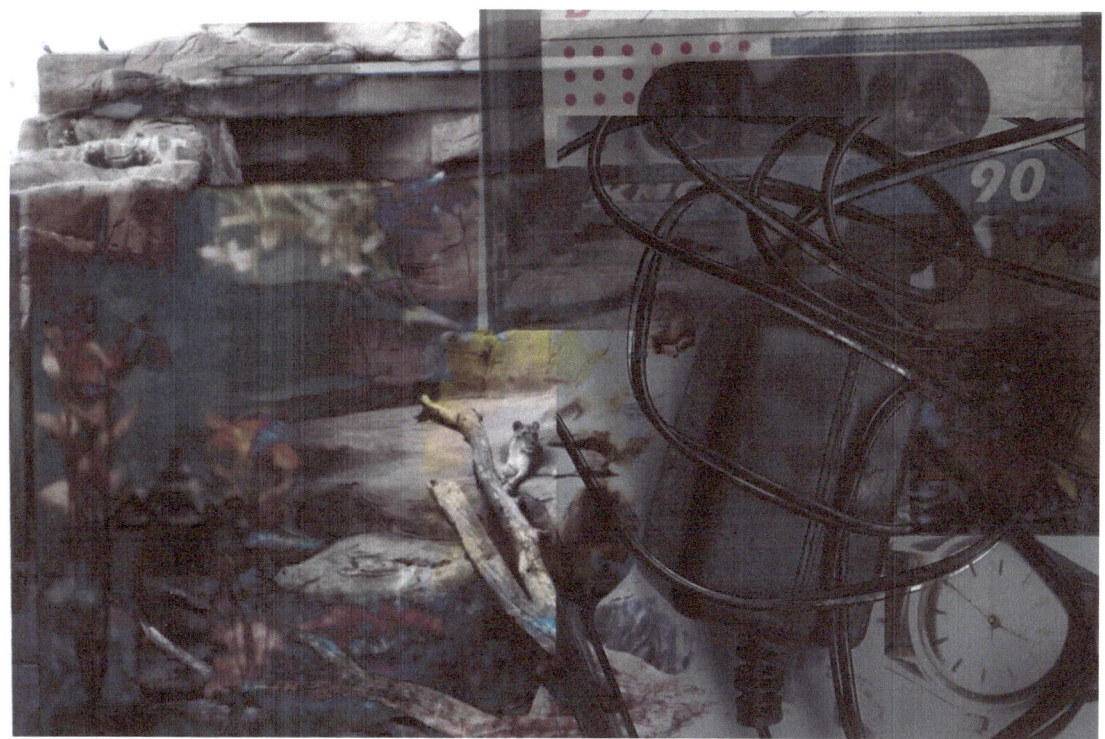

2002. "Funky town." Digital photography by Emily H. Cato (Sturgill)

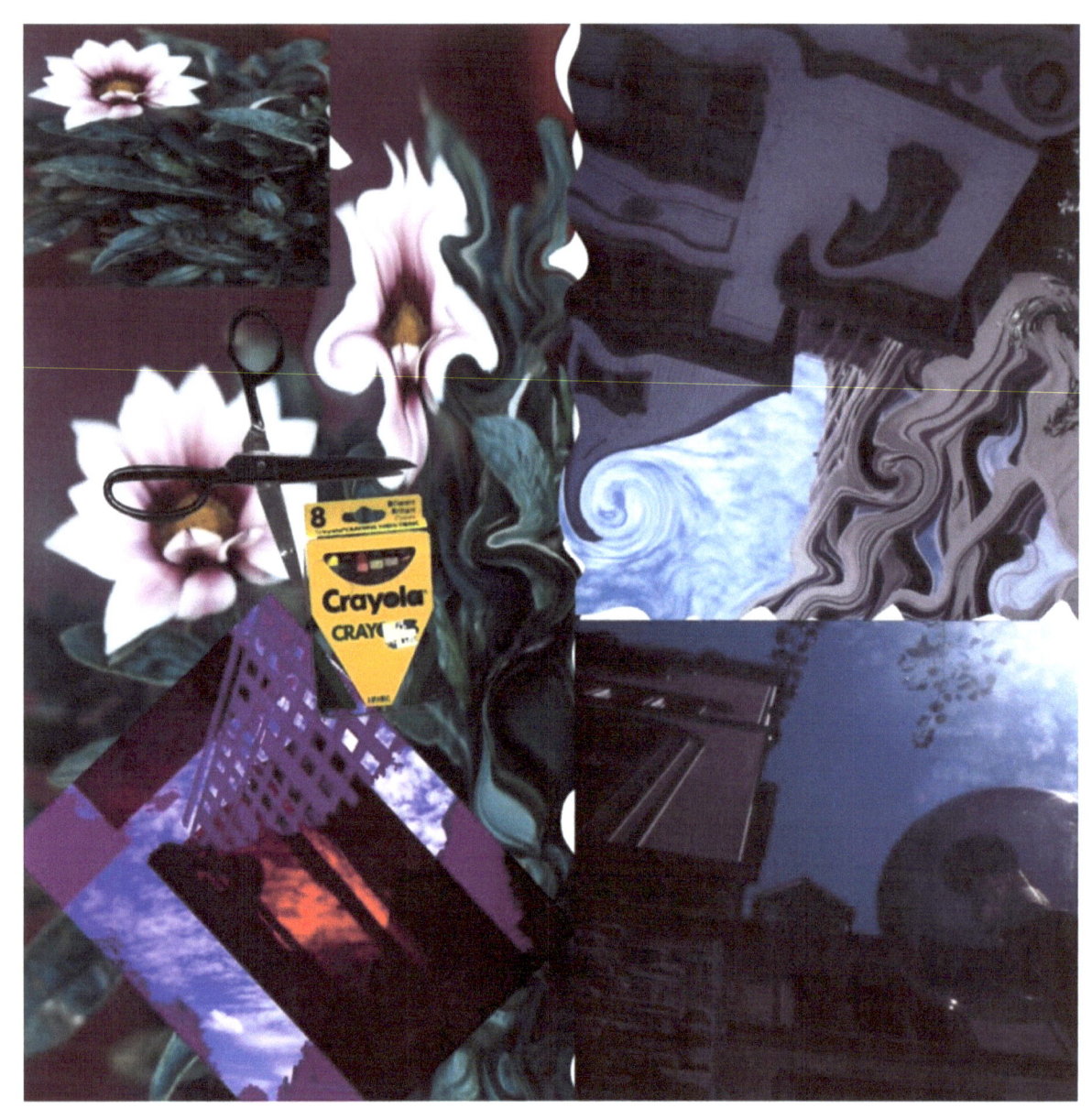

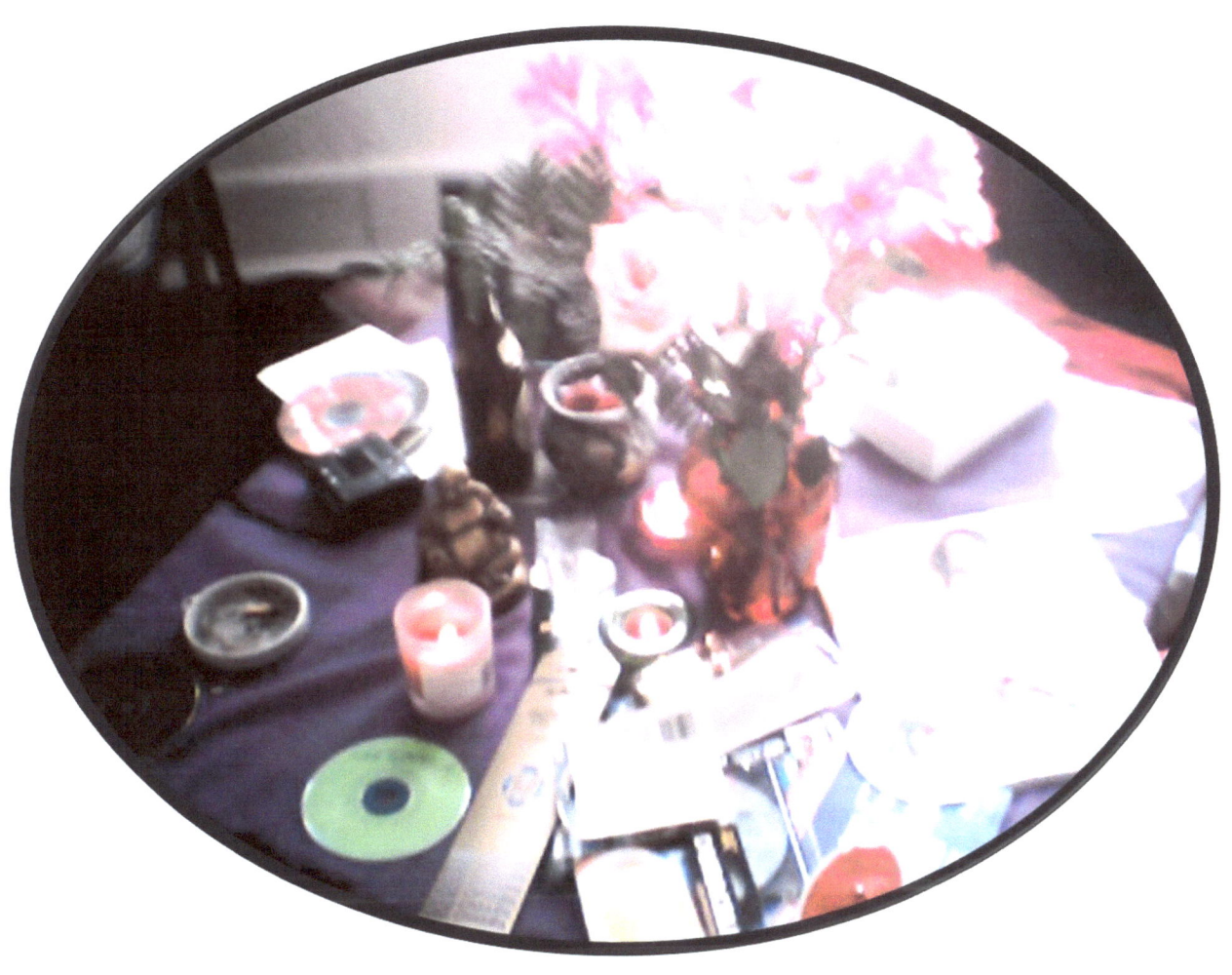

2012.Watercolor. "Still-life of mixed flowers in a Vase." By Emily H. Sturgill

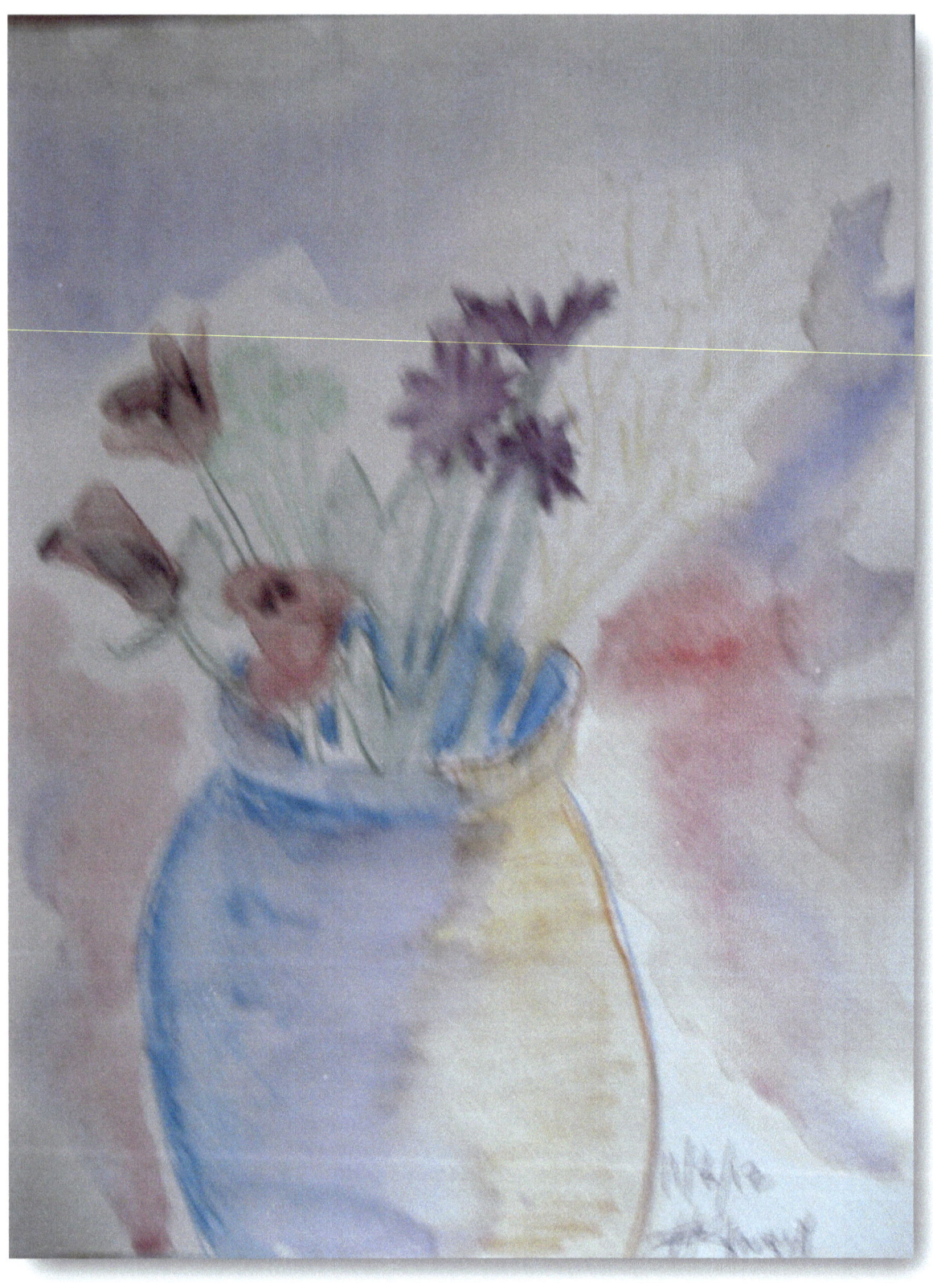

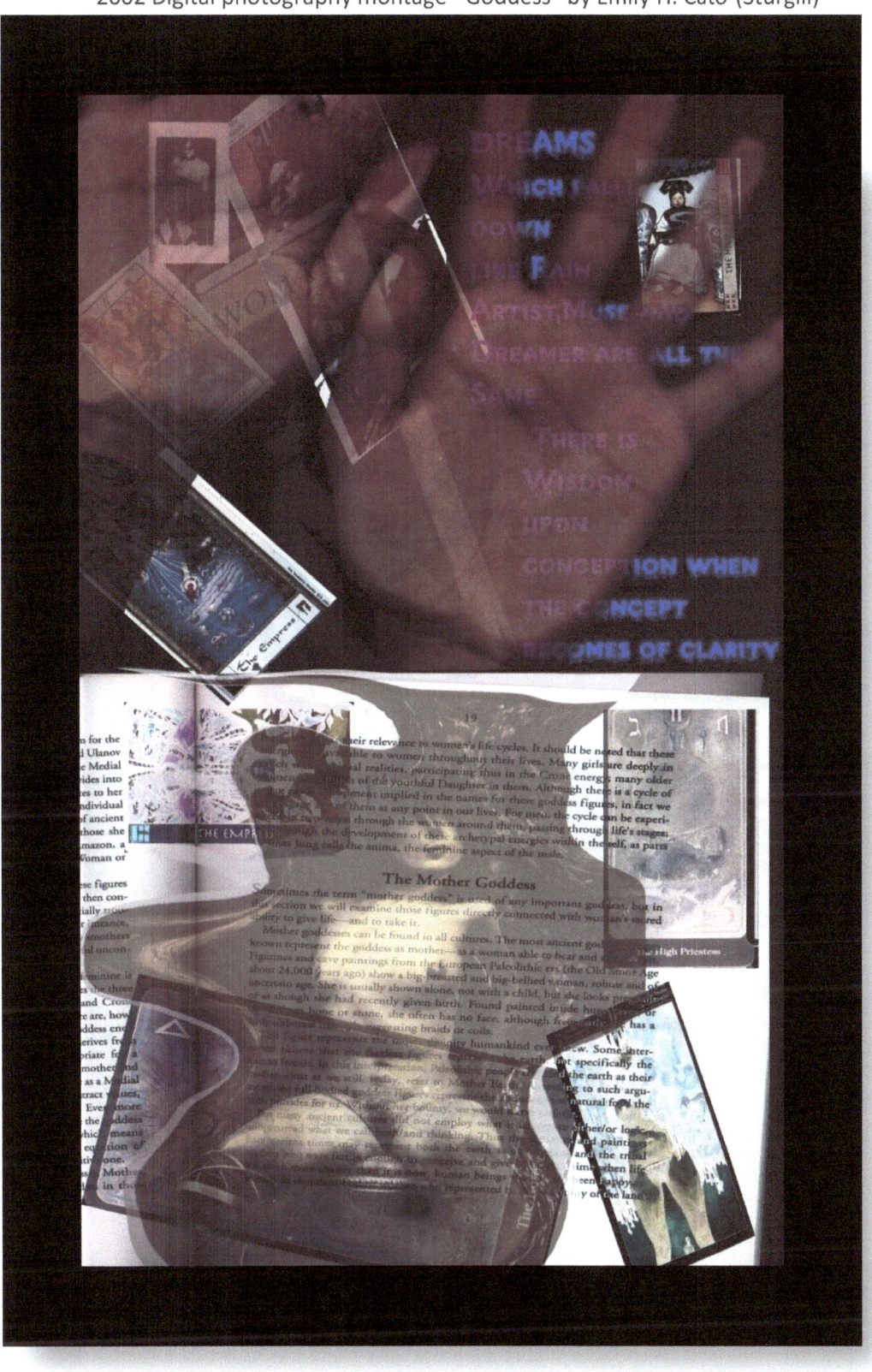

2003.Oil on canvas. "Abstraction Series painting No.2" by Emily H. Cato (Sturgill)

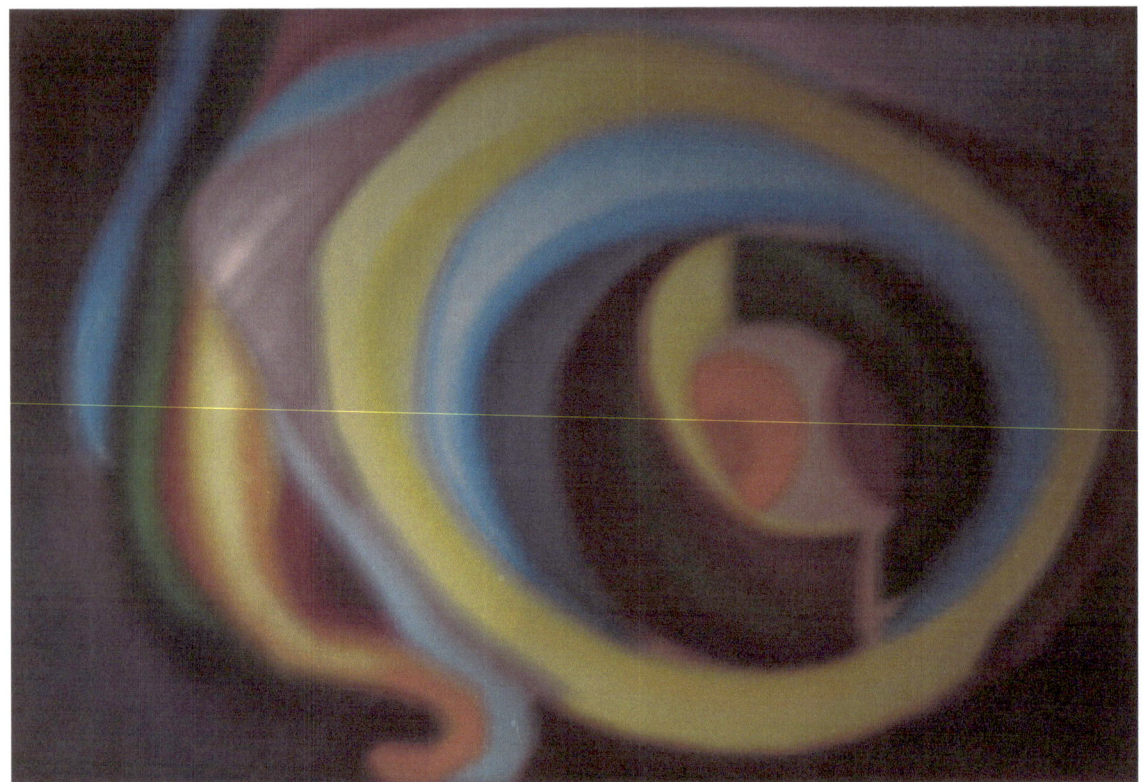

2002.Digital photography-digital collage. "Self-portrait, with man & shiba inu puppy."by Emily H.Cato (Sturgill).

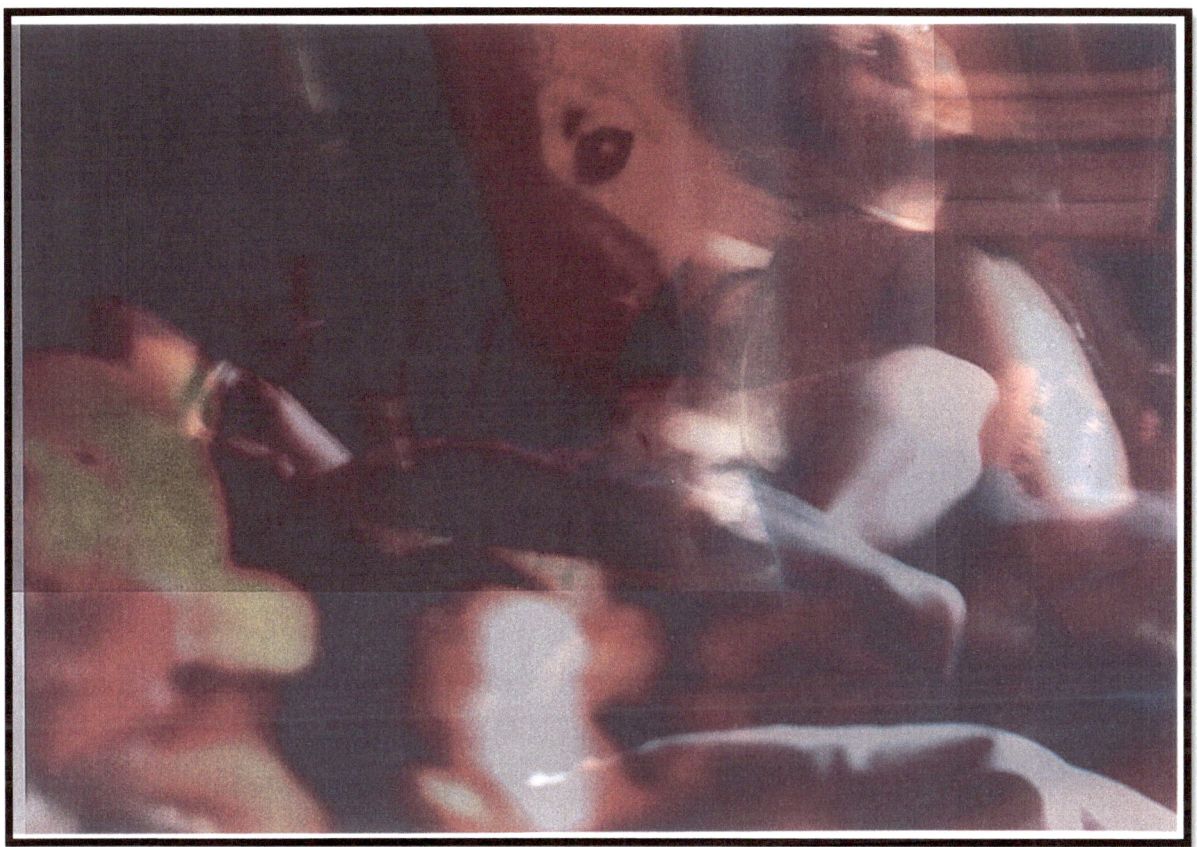

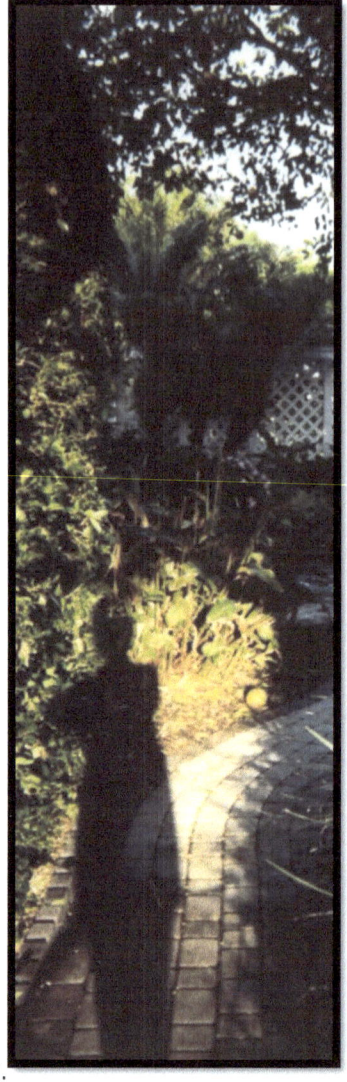

1998. Self-portrait in my sister's garden, in her backyard in Florida.

2002.Self-portrait.Digital photography & mixed media.by Emily H.Cato. (Sturgill)

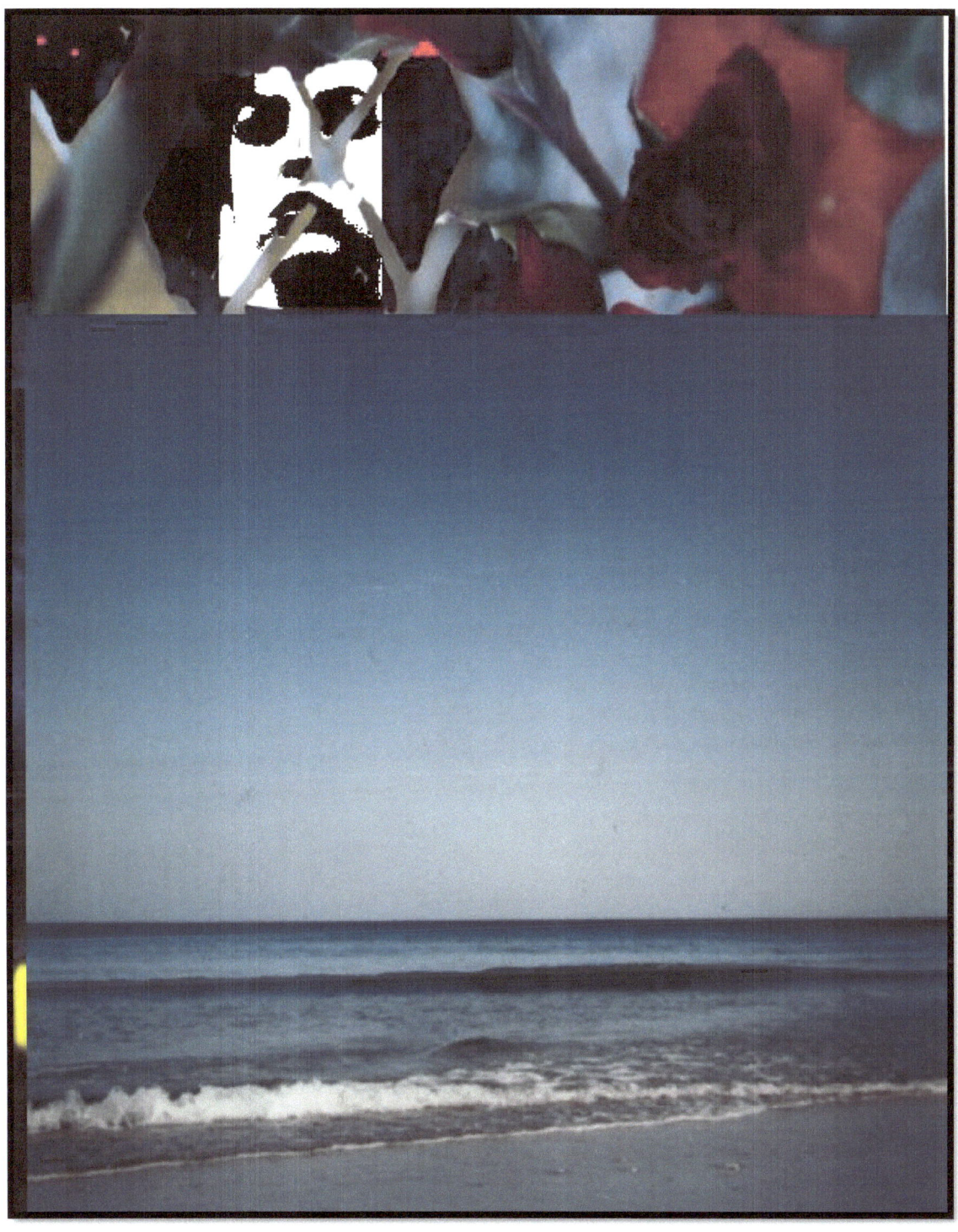

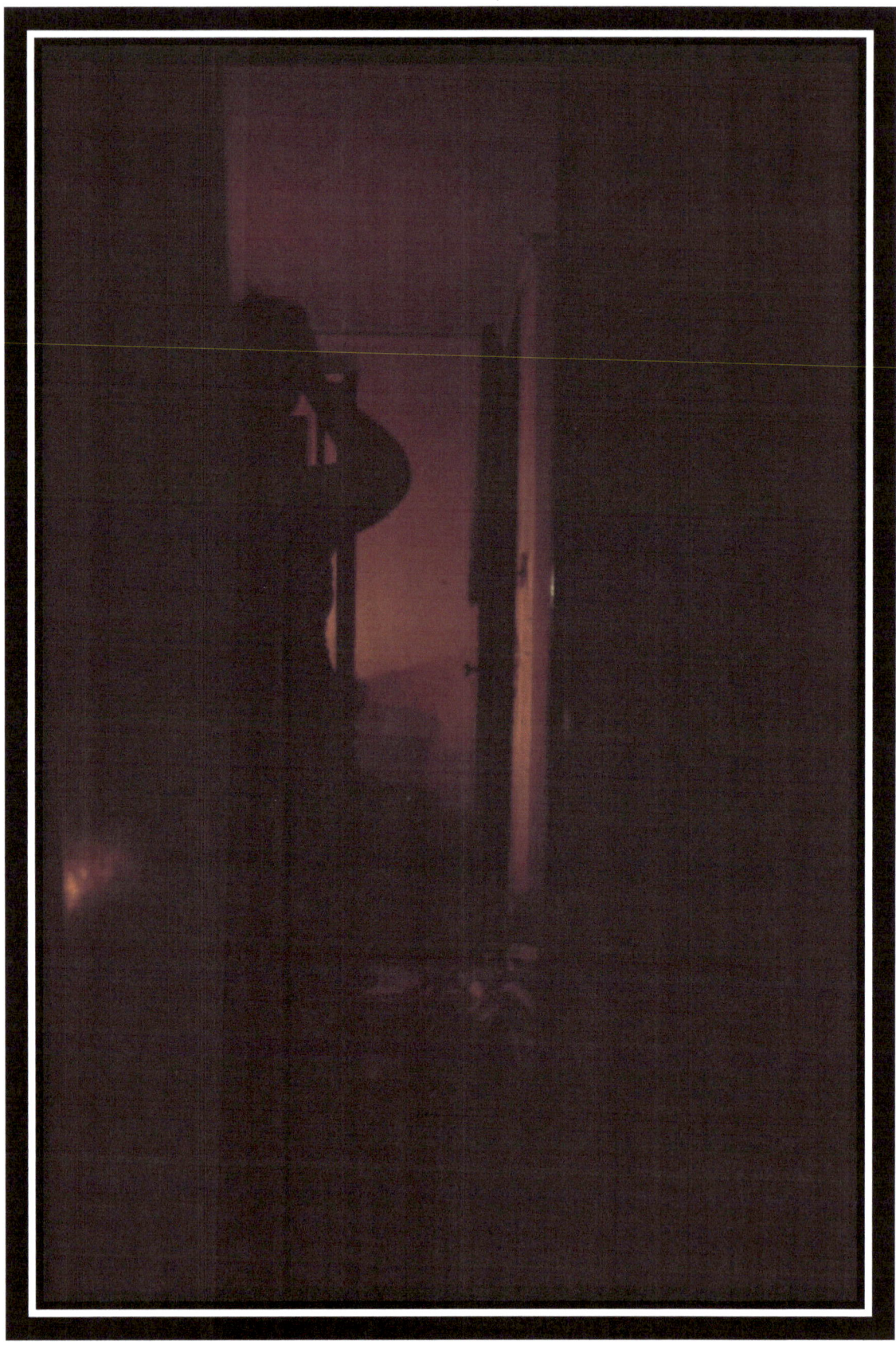

2002. Self as object. Digital photography by Emily H. Cato-(Sturgill)

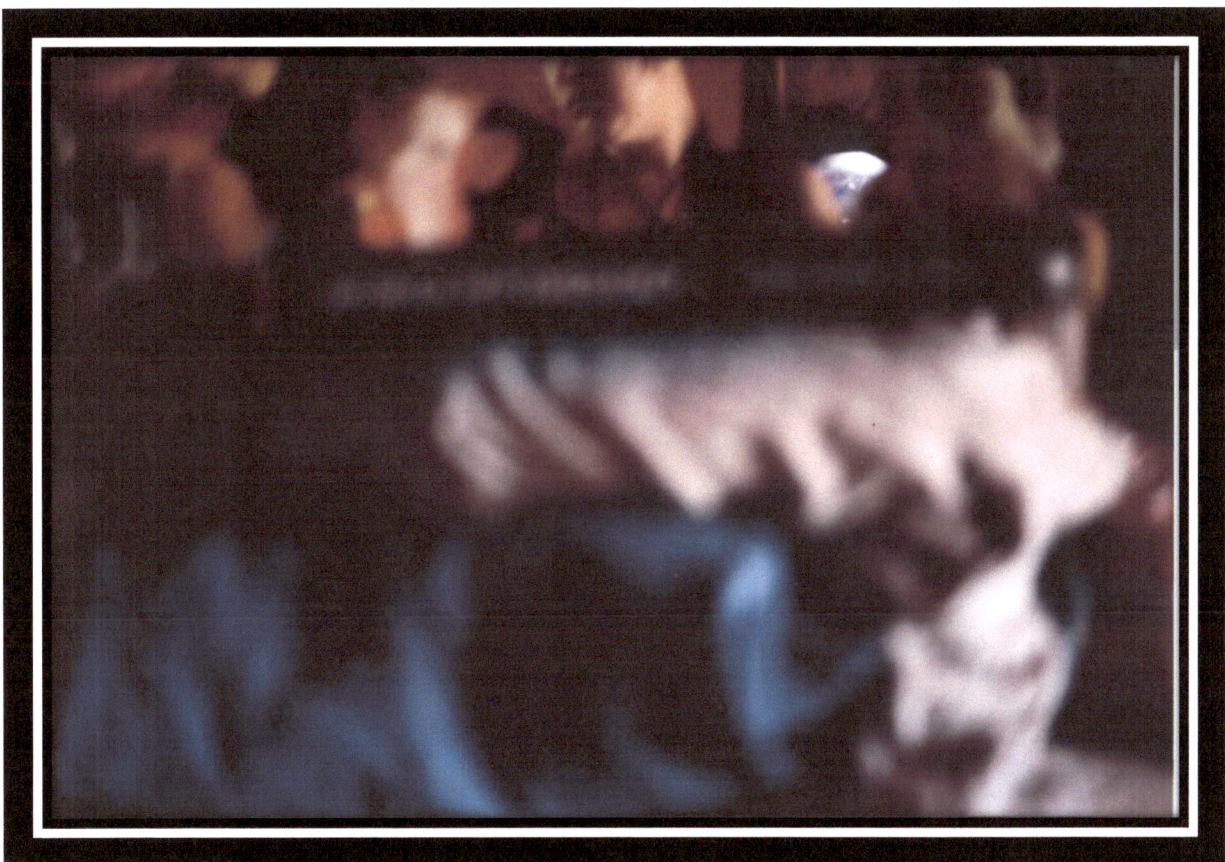

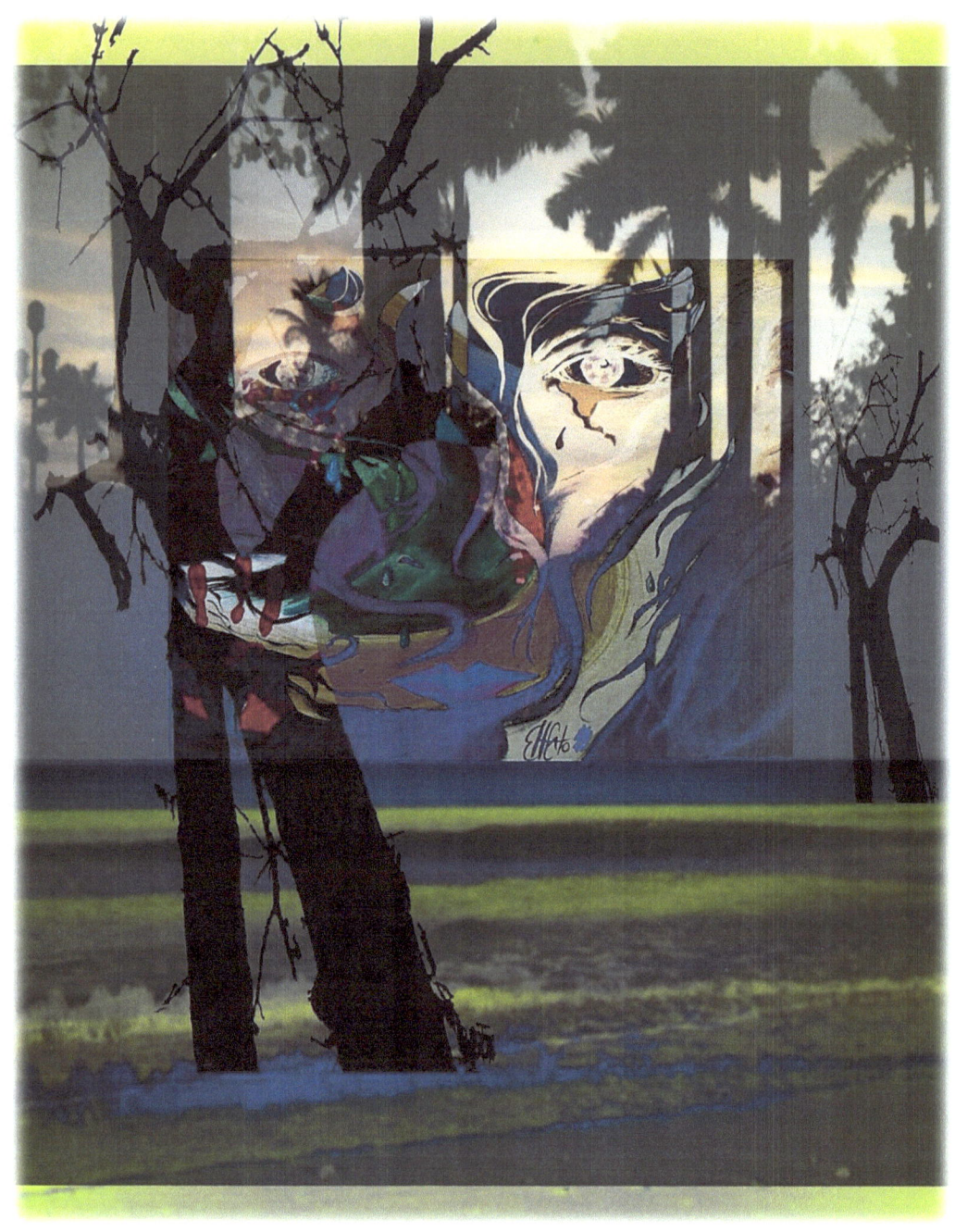

2002.Flat-planet June.Digital Montage. By Emily H. Cato (Sturgill)

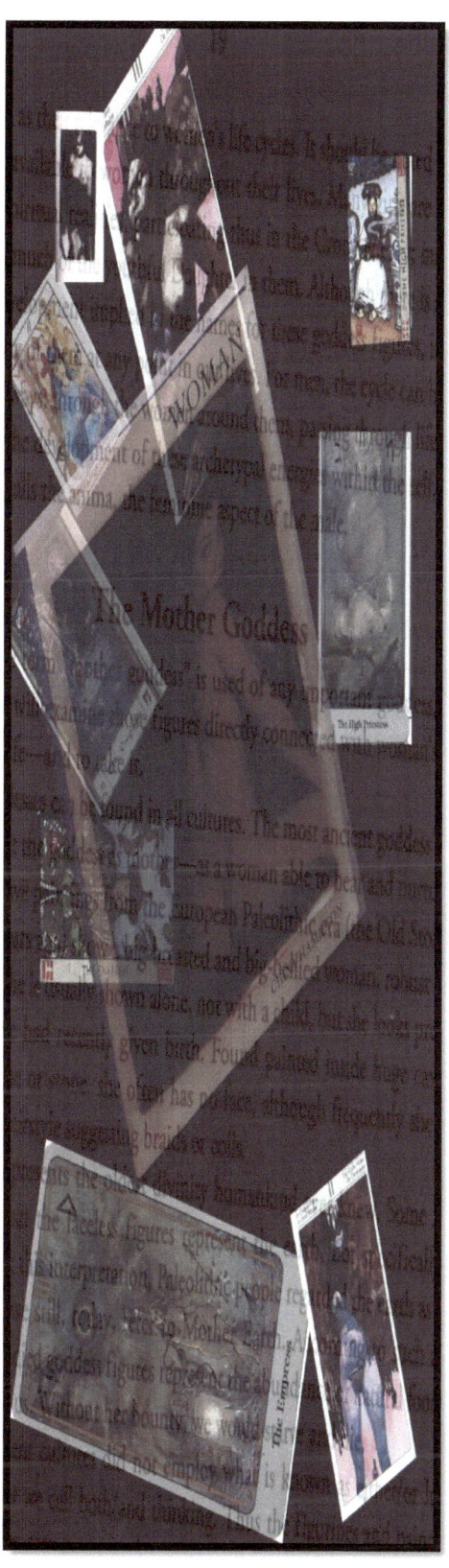

1996. "Healing hand." Acrylic paint & mixed media, on Canvas board. By Emily H. Cato (Sturgill).

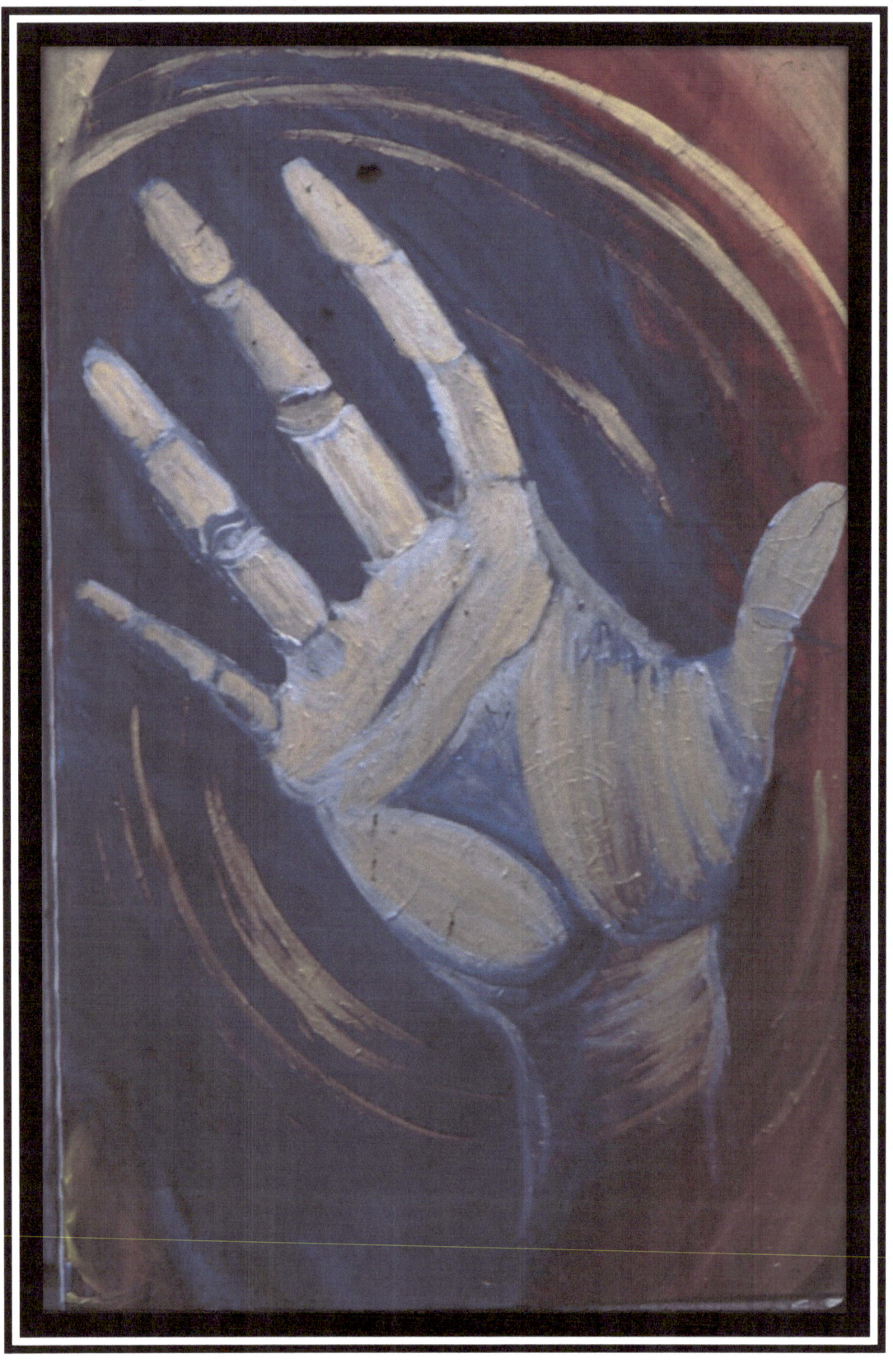

Summary- final words of advice:

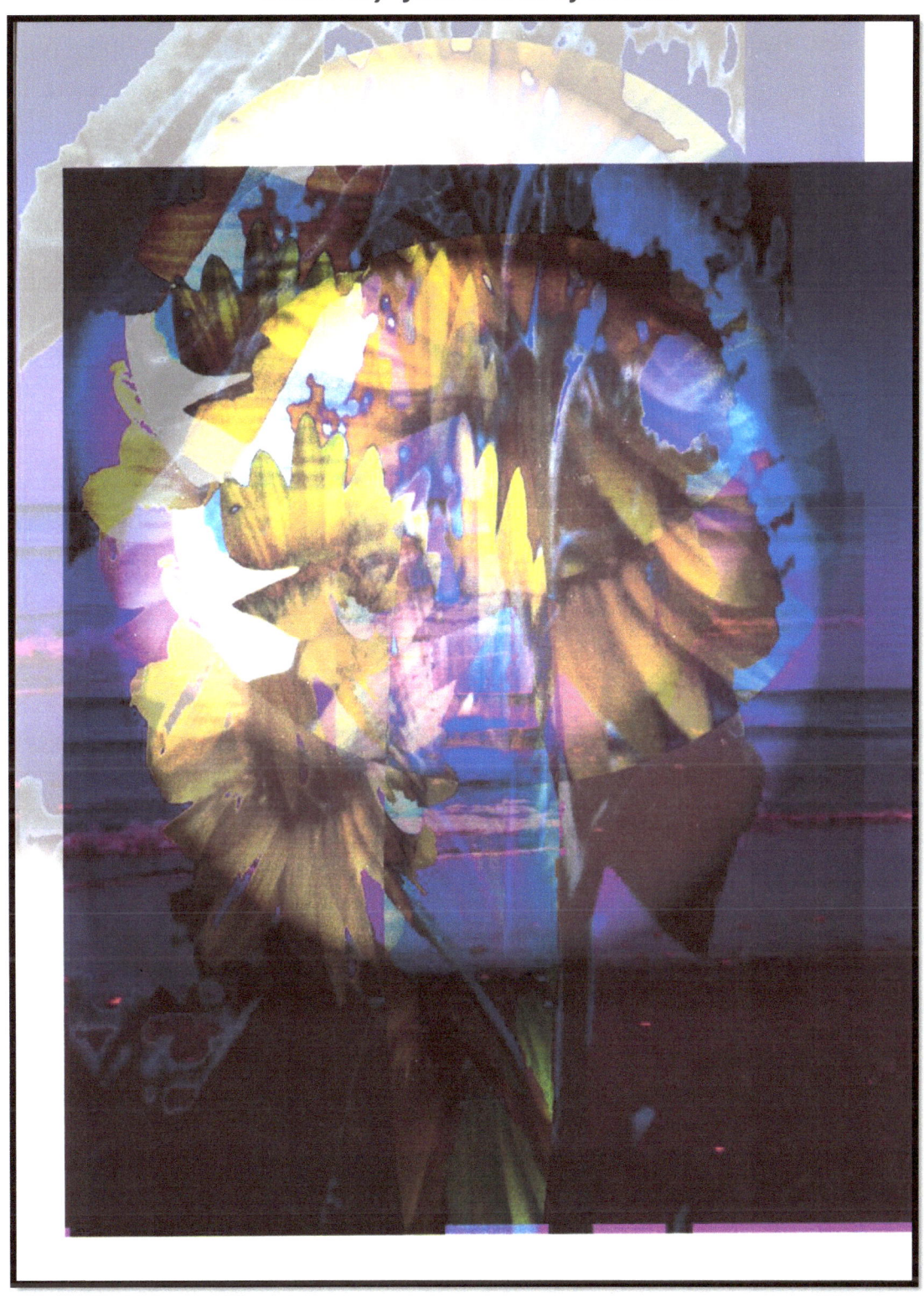

My life long love affair with the Arts has been both a blessing and a curse.

It is important in Life to find one thing, if only one, perhaps even two or three

Things you have great passion for. For me my loves have always been:

Creating Artwork, Writing poetry & listening to music-various kinds.

Another passion, I have is to help others.

To teach, to inspire, to help

To show empathy and compassion for my fellow human beings.

My bursts of creativity often cause concern for my husband.

That is because he cares a great deal and I do have mental illness.

Once I start a new project, I become very fixated and obsessive.

That is the darker secret to my Art-the curse part.

Someday, perhaps I can get a job working as an art therapist?

But for now, I am just going to focus on the housewife stuff & try not

To stress out over things beyond my control, like the current ecpnomic recession and the lack of

Employment opportunities. When the time is right, I will go back to work.

I hope you enjoyed this small sampling of artwork.

I know its not very long.

But I feel visually that the pieces flow nicely into one another.

Unlike my first volume, I decided against labeling artwork based on measurements

Of size. Many of the photography and digital photography was

Originally printed onto 8 x 10 paper, but saved as 35mm slides.

Mostly, I only have the digital records of that artwork already

Loaded onto my computer. Some of the other art varies in sizes,

However many of my older paintings have been lost or destroyed, or even given away.

That makes it much more difficult to determine sizes, please overlook this.

ACKNOWLEDGEMENTS

I would like to express gratitude and thanks to the following persons:

Michel Short, for always being so encouraging and supportive of my writing & chapbooks.

Karen Timek, for being my "bestest" friend in the entire universe. She always accepts and loves me, just for being my unique (and crazy) Self. Dean Sturgill, because he is my everything.

Erik B. Tichik & his husband, Peter Spencer, both for simply being great friends to me.

(I must add that they are my friends in separate and unique ways.)

I wish to thank The Art Experience in Pontiac MI, for giving me countless opportunities,

To lead art therapy workshops there on a contractual basis.

I wish to also Thank my Art Therapy Friends:

Julie & Mike Moreno, Pat &Marie Murray, Lindsey K., Judy Wilson,Leah Huber,Amy Rostollan Hamman, Nicole Hoida, Jen Josefosky, Gabbie Gonzales, Kate Sullivan, Holly-Feen, Rebecca Nancy Wolfe, Dr.Karen Schrugin, Meah Tweh and Megan Schmidt.

I would also like to thank some old personal friends: Tiffany Baker, Jenny Deel, Angie Abraham, Erin Oehler,Stacy Newsome-Kerr, Matthew Trectchler, Kermit Siegle, Ken Johnson and Christine Payne.

Also Family & Friends of our Family: Thank you to the following;

Tammy & Steve, Laura,Ethan &Larry, Thomas, Amy, Paul,Thalia,Steve, Sioux & Charity,Chris &Bonnie, Alice &Ken, Edy, Robert &Pam, Rell & Susan, Lisa & Christopher-all of my many nieces and nephews,my mother-in-law Debbie, and in memory of my mother Susan Ellen. I will always love and miss you. I miss you more each and everyday. But I try to treasure the good and golden memories of You-you were my "Mama." And nothing I could every write could simply sum up how amazing, fierce,funny,brilliant and

Strong you were. You were more than my Mother. You were a Hurricane, a force to be reckon with and as beautiful as the most gorgeous of sunsets. You loved in a passionate wild way. And you taught me many many things, before death stole your speech away. I will always cherish you for your strength and courage-your wisdom & your artistic abilities. I miss you very much. Someday, perhaps our paths will meet again? I dedicate this Volume of Art to you, my Mama, may you rest in peace.

Susan Ellen Cato

11/17/47-11/04/00

If you enjoyed this book,

Please feel free to give me a rating or review-

On my Author's page at Amazon.com.

Here's a link:

www.amazon.com/author/emilysturgill.

You can also see my other 15 titles there.

Author Website:

https://sexinthekitchensink.wix.com/books-by-emily

Art Therapy Website:

https://sites.google.com/site/holisticartexpressions/

My two blogs:

https://www.wordpress.com/sexinthekitchensink/feed/

https://www.dirtyfilthybutterflyblues.blogspot.com

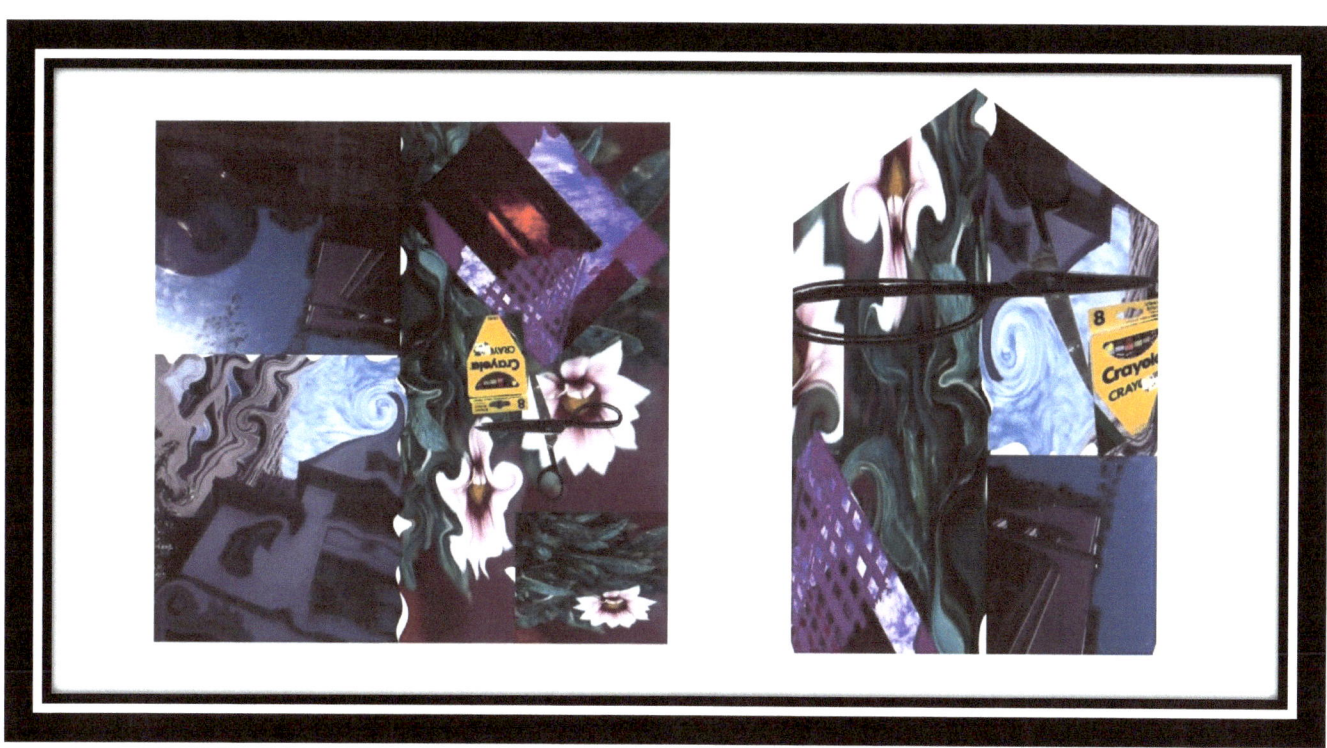

Last of all-

If any of my pictures or words inspire you, if any of the images have touched you,all I ask is one simple wish. You go somewhere quiet, and burn a single candle. May its light, shine on and enchant you. Then please, go out into the big beautiful world and make a difference in someone's life-someone less fortunate than You. Practice Random acts of Kindness, and Above all else, let your Karma guide you.

Merry meet, merry part & meet once more.

Mote it be.

Harm None.

Thank you for buying my book.

I hope you enjoyed it!

Sincerely, Emily H. Sturgill.

Sunday March 16, 2014.

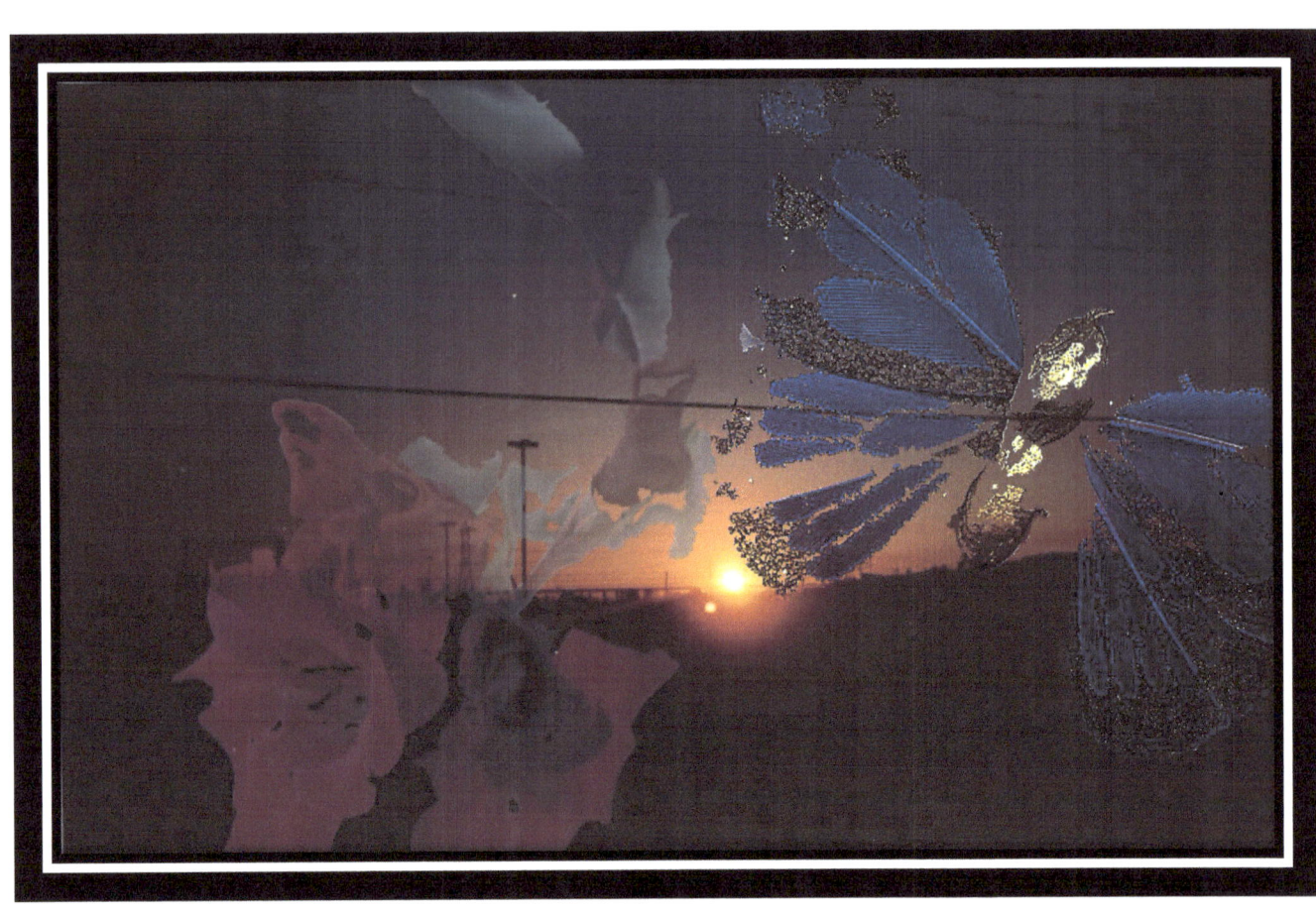

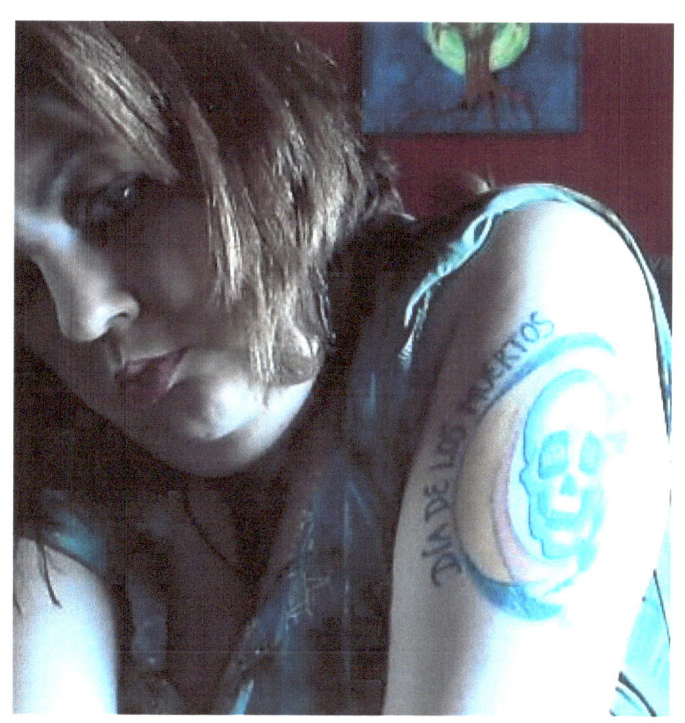

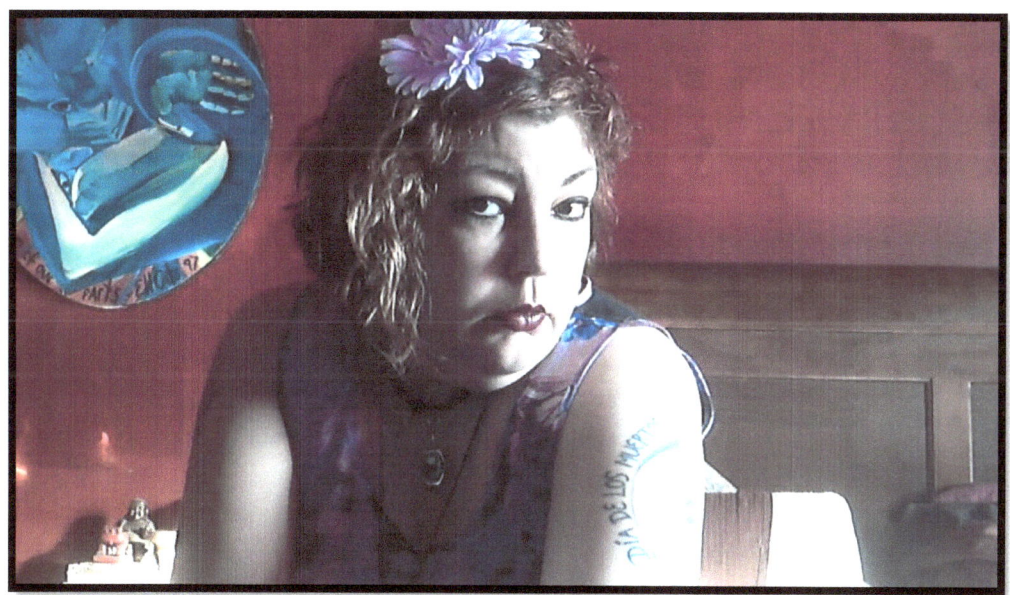

Self-portrait 2014, using web-cam

Emily H. Sturgill

THE END.

CONTACT INFO:

Emails can be sent directly to:

sexinthekitchensink@hotmail.com

www.ingramcontent.com/pod-product-compliance
Lightning Source LLC
Chambersburg PA
CBHW050815180526
45159CB00004B/1679